Introduction

Welcome to *Academic Argument by Template*. As a writer, writing tutor, and a teacher of college and university writing, I have seen many students needlessly struggle with writing for their college writing because the student failed to understand how this type of writing differs from other writing they perform.

It is critical that students understand the steps involved in preparing to write and produce academic writing because it is an unforgiving format. That is, teachers are specifically looking for key rhetorical (writing) elements in specific places, and if these elements are not there, the students' grades will suffer.

Therefore, this work has two goals. One, to provide you, the student, with a template to follow in composing your own standard academic essay and two, to explain how to insert the information to produce originally researched academic essays when trying to prove competency in English writing in colleges and universities.

You know how to write; what you need are the rhetorical skills to help you write better. This book can help.

Audience for This Book

This book is designed for you as a student doing "library research" for term papers in the introductory English classes, often called Freshman Composition 1 and 2. Often, students' previous training in writing has not prepared them to find research on their topic, narrow their topic sufficiently to produce a tight essay, analyze and synthesis those source readings, and incorporate reading from articles by other people into their own original essays.

Instead, they are taught how to find popular sources such as Wikipedia, encyclopedias, reports in the mass media (newspapers and magazines), and books that have already synthesized the work of others. These popular information sites do not adequately prepare students for academic work because they do not require the general reader to question the information and draw their own conclusions. Often these works will be geared towards summaries, as in articles discussing 'studies' that have been conducted. In an academic format these studies will present the reason for the study, background about other similar studies, the methodology used to collect information, the results from the study, and the findings of the study. When these works transcend to popular information sites, the only information left is what the study found and why it is important. The general reader is not expected to question the accuracy of the study or explore the methods used to gather the data – however the academic reader must do this.

In addition, instructors also fail to inform students about the conditions surrounding writing in college. Academic writing has specific conventions and formats that each student is expected to show he or she has mastered throughout his or her college program. Because students fail to understand the conventions, they do not know when to apply them later in their academic writing.

It is important that students realize that writing differs across disciplines, if they are to succeed. Because of their lack of awareness of conventions, students are often under the assumption that teachers grade their written assignments by how well instructors like students and not on whether or not students have incorporated the necessary conventions for the paper the students are attempting to produce. In some instances this may be true. Nevertheless, students do not need to rely on the personal goodwill of the instructor if they learn to master the academic essay.

Students who have already finished the two classes needed for their Core Competency in English will also benefit from this book if they have not previously received instruction on how to prepare critical analysis of published research on theoretical premises or have not received instruction on what required rhetorical elements are necessary for the academic argument paper.

Finally, those who are preparing to write academic essays (middle school and high school students) can benefit from the information provided in this book because understanding the form and requirements will enable them to produce essays that will allow them to CLEP out of classes to save money *and* will allow them to produce essays for publication in journals.

While most students who have not yet entered or have just entered college think of publishing in a journal dedicated to a specific field as something as remote as taking a ride on the space shuttle, increasingly if you want to be considered as a serious scholar (an A student) in college, students need to look for publishing opportunities as soon as they enter school.

Ten or twenty years ago, publishing this soon was unheard of. However, with the increase in the sheer numbers of students entering college and obtaining degrees, those who want to find the best viable job market after they have their bachelor's degree need to consider publishing early. Moreover, the increase in bachelor degrees has also resulted in an increased interest in students continuing for a higher degree in the form of a master's or doctorate's degree. With the increased competition students have to do more than show they received their bachelor's degree. Many schools are looking for students to publish and attend conferences as they would if they were already a master's or doctorate's level student.

For all these reasons, mastering the academic argument paper will put you on the path to success!

Unique Features

The following features make this book unique as a writing guide for teaching analytical writing to you, the student:

- The book focuses on writing your own critical essays of original research instead of reading works by professional writers.
- There are no essays for you to read and infer the process from; the template method tells you exactly what should be introduced and where it should be.

To Students

This guide is to help you understand and write standard academic argument essays. While the overview briefly mentions other writing genres students need to know and master in the course of the education, this book focuses only on the most commonly assigned standard argument essay, which encourages the most creativity and flexibility on the part of students.

The essential points of the standard argument essay are covered in the first section and are broken down into three chapters: an overview of the writing process, a template for the standard academic essay, and a chapter discussing how argument is incorporated into this assignment.

Following the essential points you need to understand in composing this type of assignment is a detailed look at the writing process and how to ensure your paper is adequately completed to get the best grade.

No writing guide can deliver an A on your paper; however, by understanding clearly what the instructor expects you to be able to do in order to complete the standard academic essay, you will be on the road to success.

To Instructors

Many colleges and universities design Writing Programs as a one-fits all model. Students from all disciplines are placed into a class that is taught by an instructor who typically only know writing skills for the College of English in which they earned their degree. The instructor, upon earning a master's degree, is handed a textbook in one of two formats. Either it is genre based with essays showing narrative, compare/contrast, process, and other genres of writing, or the textbook is based on writing with sources. Each of these textbooks will have an introductory section with the same writing process detailed: brainstorming, research (if necessary), first draft, revision, proof-reading, submission. This is a process that overlies all writing, but it fails to explain to the students how they should visual their final product from such broad theories.

In addition, many students fail to find this process helpful. It is not that they do not use the process, but that they use it so specifically already that generalities are of no help for them in refining their own writing skills. In few other classes, except college level writing, do we ask students to 'dump' all they know about a subject to master it. Moreover, it is completely unnecessary. Students who follow the templates of various forms of academic writing will be able to realize what their writing skills lack as they work on producing proficient essays.

While the goals of 'one-fits-all' writing programs are admirable, many instructors are only able to cover the traditional content in their courses and have little time to truly teach writing skills individually. Generally, this means students not following the rhetorical rules receive low grades and continue doing so because they cannot translate the general theory into the particular writing or that the student is sent to a tutor to receive assistance. While this may sound helpful, most colleges and universities do not hire writing teachers to tutor. Tutoring can be done by anyone who passed the writing course with an A. Having received an A does not guarantee that the student will understand how to analyze writing difficulties and disabilities in other students. Also although the A students have *done* well, they may not know *why* they did well. Nevertheless, these students are often the only help a struggling student has because the pay of tutors is so low that instructors will not continue working in this area long.

A lack of knowledge can also be a problem for the instructors as well. Although writing is said to be a vital skill for students, it is almost always taught by 'inexperienced' teachers. The people who fill the instructor slots in these sections are most often scholarship students who have little or no teaching experience and part-time, temporary adjunct positions that pay low wages. Both of these categories make teaching writing difficult. For the student, other classes take up the time of the student in order for them to receive their own diploma. Even when they recognize a student is having problems there is little they can do about it, other than refer them to a tutor who is, again, just educationally just above the struggling student. For the adjunct, things are little better. Most cannot live above poverty level on the wages they receive from teaching, which means in addition to accepting at least five classes each semester, they will most likely have another part-time job. It is not that the adjuncts won't care. They are simply over worked.

Other factors influence the teaching of writing, too. For instance, many of the instructors never took more than one course on the theories of teaching writing or the practice of teaching writing. For most disciplines, the instructor at the college level must have passed no less than five courses in the subject for which they are allowed to lecture and teach, but this rule does not apply to the teaching of writing. Many writing teachers have no idea why things like journals are encouraged or how they should be incorporated correctly within a writing class.

Often these factors of inadequate teacher training and low-paying jobs mean that students are not taking the Freshman Composition courses to learn how to write academic essays. They are only being judged that they already know how to write academic essays.

Such instructors will find this book helpful because of the concrete steps presented for students to follow in the writing process, which also makes it possible for students to use the book on their own. Teachers who know how to 'naturally' write well will find ideas on how to *teach* writing to students who are struggling, rather than expecting these students to infer and to absorb good writing skills from essays crafted by professional writers. Used as a supplement, this book will help instructors with struggling students achieve better results by showing what elements students need to shape and craft their writing into academic writing.

Acknowledgements

I would like to thank my students over the past ten years. They taught me more about writing than I ever learned from the university. I began my teaching life at the university, having never taught any class before or been instructed in the art of teaching and lesson plans. I realized quite quickly a master's degree was not adequate preparation to teach the essential skill of writing.

Moreover, there seemed to be no general consensus about what 'writing' was to be taught in the Freshmen writing course. Professors for other disciplines complained that their students passed the writing class but still could not write a passable essay for other disciplines. Even English teachers had no consensus about what was required. Most assigned a 'one-shot writing assignment,' a term coined by (Kamhi-Stein) in 1997. This is where the instructor gives an assignment using a prompt ("Write about an event that changed your life"). The paper is given as a specific task. As the semester progresses, it will include library research, and the quality of the paper is supposed to depend on the care with which students follow steps of the writing process. However, most of these steps are never checked by the instructor. Even those instructors who do check them cannot ensure that their prompt will spark the creative energy needed by students to feel emotionally invested in their paper. As a result papers are often dry and bland, lifeless.

In addition, students do not know how to actually do the creative part of coming up with a research topic and being able to narrow their topic down appropriately. Most of the students I have taught have been challenged by just being allowed to be interested in what interests them. Unfortunately, most have not learned how to limit their paper sufficiently so that they are not producing a dissertation length work for class. Instructors who complain about students underwriting papers and not caring about topics, should allow more time for students to find topics. They will find the same students are now eager to write longer papers and instructors only have to set a cap on how many pages they are willing to read.

These students have also taught me that students are changing. I started teaching the group known as the Millennials. These students graduated in 2000. Unlike older, nontraditional students, this group understands how to use computers and how to research information using popular sources. Indeed, they are often much more adept at this than their instructors. However, they do not understand scholarly databases, which are the core of academic writing. They do not know how to critically analyze and synthesize academic sources and primary sources. They are used to find secondary sources that present summaries only. They also often fail to question the authority of the writer. If it was published, they consider it good enough.

The Generation Xers are also different. Like the Millennials, they understand popular sources. They often blog, tweet, and facebook. While their writing skills are often good, they do not understand the importance of multiple examples and topic sentences in academic writing. Let's face it, in the cyber world these elements are not considered of vital importance. Even Technical Writing and Business Communication textbooks will tell students of writing, 'just the facts, ma'am'. This means that this group needs context to understand why their essays need to have what other types of writing do not require. Generation Xers are more focused on wanting guided processes.

Being on the cusp of the Baby Boomers and the Millennials, my writing teachers' assignments would be something like, 'write a five page essay due by this date.' We were expected to find the topic, limit it, and choose which genre would be best to make the work fresh and exciting. We understood without being explicitly told that if we needed help we were to ask before the due date of the paper, and that we could turn the paper in early but not late. Generation Xers do not understand these unstated rules of the game. Older instructors will find that this group wants to talk about their steps in their papers instead of the reading assignments. Their only interest in a reading assignment will be how it will advance their particular paper.

This is a challenge for the writing instructor. I found over the last ten years I have been teaching that I have had to constantly revise how I am presenting information. Writing teachers have to maintain a constant dialogue with their students in order to be able to assist them. I thank my students for their insights, helpfulness, and understanding.

Most of all I thank them for reminding me that as a teacher I need to remember they already know how to write, what they need is instruction in how to write better.

Errors and omissions are my own responsibility; mea culpa.

Feedback

Writing improves with feedback from others. I welcome your comments and reflections on this work. I am especially interesting in suggestions for improving this writing guide. You can write me using the address of the publisher Independent Scholar Press, P.O. Box 2907, Universal City, Texas, 78148, or by emailing me at rlsmithwriter@aol.com.

R.L. Smith

San Antonio, Texas

Dedication

For my parents and their unwavering love.

Table of Contents

Introduction   Page | xv

Chapter One: Writing Academic Papers: An Overview

Chapter Two: Template for Creating the Standard Academic Essay

Chapter Three: Understanding Argument and the Standard Academic Essay

DISCLAIMER:

There are no express or implied warranties or representations for the accuracy or completeness of this work. This work is sold with the understanding that the author and publisher are not engaged in rendering legal, advice-based, or other professional services. If professional service is required, the services of a competent professional should be sought. Neither the author or publisher should be liable for damages arising herefrom.

The Academic Essay—By Template

Chapter 1

Writing Academic Papers: An Overview

In this book, you will be learning how to write academic essays using primary and secondary sources. In addition, you will be learning how different academic disciplines have different requirements, which you will have to be able to adapt to as you progress towards completing your bachelor's degree. By far the most common academic essays you will encounter as freshman, sophomore, and juniors are mixed genre essays (ones that combines many rhetorical genres, or types of writing like compare/contrast, process, cause/effect); the most common type of essays for thesis and honors papers is the empirical study, a type of essay to explain how independent research was carried out.

This chapter begins with an overview of the types of genre essays you may encounter in Freshman Composition I: the narrative, persuasive, process, compare and contrast, cause and effect, definition, problem and solution, research, argument, and empirical. These genres are followed by a brief discussion of the writing process you will need to incorporate into your writing to succeed at academic writing. Although a full discussion of these genres are not provided in this book, this discussion serves as an overview for the rest of the book because without understanding the genres, you cannot properly include them into a mixed essay.

This chapter assumes you already know how to write and have in fact already written some compositions. It also assumes that you what you lack are rhetorical skills not always taught with writing: how to talk about writing, its genres and their purposes. Whether you are writing a single genre essay (one overall pattern-type of writing, like a definition paper, or a mixed genre essay (many genres used in paragraph form within the overall essay), the purposes for each genre remains the same and keeps the same requirements. While the structure of the genres is discussed in an overview provided here, the purpose of this book is not to cover all possible writing assignments—it is devoted exclusively to the argument mixed-genre essay, aka the standard academic essay.

What is the Standard Academic Essay?

The standard academic essay is seldom defined in a Freshman Composition course. It is expected that students will acquire a unique, sophisticated writing voice as they progress through their college courses.

That they will assimilate the meaning of good academic writing, without their being told. It is not, however, necessary to guess at what instructors want when they assign an essay.

For this type of writing assignment, students are expected to compose and arrange a mixed-genre essay that discusses points relevant to their claim or argument.

That is all — in a sense. The standard academic essay does require students think about how to arrange points they want to make in favor of their claim and how to present the fact that others may disagree with their claim. It sounds simple because it is.

Officially, academic writing is a form of essay used by specialists in scholarly fields. It uses

✓ Specialized language of a particular discipline
  o Oedipus complex
  o Onomatopoeia
✓ Long and intricate sentence structure
✓ In-depth analysis, not quick, easy, or general
✓ Makes an argument

In order to be performing academic writing, you must

1) define the situation that calls for a response
2) demonstrate timeliness

3) establish investment
4) understand what the reader values, thinks, and believes
5) support your arguments with reasons
6) provide an argument that is the careful expression of an idea based on reasoning—not shooting down opponents

The Research Paper Misunderstanding.

Most commonly this assignment presents itself as a research paper or argument paper. These categories are really one. Calling a paper a research paper ensures that the student recognizes and understands that the student needs to incorporate information that the student has read about the topic he or she will write about. Students often mistake this type of assignment. They believe that their research paper has nothing to prove—that they are only being asked to regurgitate what they have read. This is not true. The research paper is more than just informing their reader about a collection of facts. If that were all, there would be no point to writing a research paper at all. Instead, students could just collect citation information and pass it along, or at most complete an annotated bibliography with summaries of what they read for their reader.

The Argument Paper Misunderstanding.

Students presented with the task of producing an argument paper believe they are being asked to write about controversial public issues, like gay marriage, immigration policies, and the occupy movement. They interpret argument as 'to fight' about something, not to discuss it. However, the goal of an argument essay is to bring a topic into conversation with others who study the subject. The goal is not to belittle, or rant, or bully the reader into changing an opinion. This type of argument is an explanation of why a claim, or position, is valid or worthy of thought.

By focusing on topics that appear as controversial in everyday society, students find it difficult to separate personal opinion from informed study. Teachers who dangle topics like discussions of gay rights in front of their students give the appearance to students that individual opinions on the subject are valued. These students are often hurt when they find that their opinions really are not valued. Instead, the teacher really wants the student to tell him or her what other academics think.

Secondly, these current topics lead to another major problem. Students present their arguments the same way they would discuss the topic with their friends, family, and people they meet in the street. This is to say, they make unsupported claims. They will say things like:

- The U.S. should deport immigrants who come to this country illegally.
- Abortion is against the Bible and should be stopped.
- BP caused the oil spill in the Gulf Coast and should be forced to clean up the mess.
- Guns are dangerous and should not be allowed on college campuses.
- The NRA are vigilantes who patrol the border to harass poor, working-class people looking for work.

Statements like theses will be translated into their writing. These are debatable issues. The problem arises that for an argument to be made, the student needs to provide three things:

- ❖ The claim
- ❖ The warrant
- ❖ The support

However, in everyday conversations we do not provide our warrants or our supports (these will be discussed in Chapter Three). We only make our claims.

Often our claims are phrased in a way to protect our opinions from attack. For instance, if I said, "I think President Obama is mishandling the Iran War," it is clearly my opinion. If I made the statement around friends, I may be expecting them to support what I say, or even know they will support what I say without my having to explain why I believe what I do. Most people who do not know me would not step in and challenge my statement. There is little reason to because of the way I phrased my attack of President Obama. It is my personal opinion—I think. One of the inherent rights of an American is freedom of speech. Tacking the phrase on to a claim 'I think' or 'I believe' is often recognized as expressing my right to free expression. Although others may not agree with my belief they are unlikely to challenge it, and there can be no real discussion of the issues surrounding Obama's actions and his reason for those actions regarding the Iran War.

This short-hand way of presenting arguments appears in all kinds of contexts. If someone asks you what you thought of *The Lord of the Rings* or *War Horse*, you might respond, "I liked it. You should go see it," particularly if you know the other person has not seen the movie. On one hand, we don't want to give away an ending like the blabbermouth cartoon women in theater previews.

We don't provide the underlying reasons that lead us to our claim.

On the other hand, academic arguments require, nay demand, we provide the steps that lead us to our claim. The argument should reveal our thought process. Who we value as creditable, what we believe, and how the pieces of information that we gather culminate in a single point of view that others have not understood or seen or have not been able to express as well as we can.

An Introduction to Rhetorical Writing Genres

Why focus on Rhetorical Writing Genres, if I will only be using the mixed genre model or the empirical research model?

Unfortunately, it is not possible. What Freshman Composition I is designed to do when it is taught using single genre essays is to ensure students understand what the reader expects in academia when certain rhetorical genres are employed by the writer (you).

Your grade and your papers.

The most important thing about rhetorical patterns is that you will be graded upon how well you use them, although you will seldom be told this as you progress through your college courses. Partly, this occurs because teachers are taught to grade written assignments using one of two methods: the holistic and the rubric.

The holistic method.

In the holistic method the teacher collects all the papers at the same time (meaning later papers will not be tolerated or that there will be point deductions for having to read the paper separately to ensure that the student is not given a higher grade. The teacher then secludes him- or herself with the papers and reads them straight through. Based on this reading the teacher will place the paper in a pile labeled A, B, C, D, or F. Some teachers will make a few notations along the way; therefore, never having to read the paper again. Others will re-read the paper and justify their first reading with comments. If their gut reaction to the paper was that it was crappy, they will look for things to mark on the paper to provide a reason for the student receiving a poor grade.

Grades will depend upon the mood of the teacher when they are grading, especially if they are not going to re-read the paper, and the order in which the paper appears in the pile. Some papers will seem brilliant by what they are placed next to, and vice versa.

In this method teachers are judging the initial students by what former students turned in to them and later students by how the other class members are doing. It works like a bell-curve. A few will be obviously better writers than their classmates. These one or two students will be As. Depending on grammar and digressions, the B and C students will be marked. Then organization and the ability to stick to a central point will separate the D and F papers students produce.

This method, the most common one that I am aware of, means that if you had been in another class you would receive a different grade for the same papers. And there is nothing you can do about it. You do not get to see the final results of the class.

The rubric method.

This method is gaining favor because it gives the appearance of fair grading. In this method you will be given a model that shows how the instructor will take off points, hopefully before you have to submit the assignment. If you receive it after, it is just another justification method for the grade you received that was graded holistically. Indeed, it may be anyway, but a rubric established before the assignment is due gives students a better chance of fair grading for the same problems among classmates. It is not, nevertheless, perfect.

The idea behind the rubric is to provide point values to each part of an essay. Things that are missed are subtracted until you receive your grade.

Regrettably, an essay is a high level cognitive (thinking) piece. It is not reducible to the sum of its parts. A brilliant essay may have a strong dominant point, but never be explicitly stated. In the rubric method, the ability to point to this feature (the written thesis statement) and say here it is takes precedence over what can be inferred (an unstated thesis).

Moreover, C and lower students will find the rubric more restrictive than good. Instead of focusing on changing a few things in their writing, they will look at the sheer number of things and give up.

Studies have shown that students should only deal with three writing issues at one time, if they want to be successful at eliminating their problems and improving their writing. The rubric does not accommodate this thinking.

How will this affect my grade?

If you cannot grab the instructor's interest in your paper by your introduction, your paper will be going downhill from there. This is a very specific niche writing. You must not only conform to the expectations of a specific assignment but also present your information in such a way the instructor is interested.

Teachers will be unwilling to change the grade later. After all, they would really have to recall the papers distributed and re-read them to ensure your paper was really at the correct level of your classmates. Worse, if they have spent hours marking all of your mechanical errors to subtract points, they will not be willing to listen to a grade change because you wasted their time with errors you didn't bother to fix which took up their time and allowed them to justify the first score they gave you.

What Are the Rhetorical Genres of Writing?

Narration.

Narration takes many forms in the Freshman Composition courses. All of these forms, however, focus only on your ability to show you can group information into sub-sections to create groups of information that are alike, limit your subject to key features, and write information clearly and entertainingly.

The entertaining part traditionally stumps students. Many disciplines do not ask students to re-invent the wheel. Therefore, the ability to present the information in a manner that people will read it will increasingly be imperative in your ability to get good grades. This means you have to think more creatively to ensure the teacher wants to reader your paper, not just that you have presented information correctly.

Focus on you:

Personal Narrative: tells a story about an incident that happened to you over a short period of time and had an important effect on your life.

Personal Essay: this is an extended narrative or a phase autobiography that covers an important period of your life. The difference from the work above is that you will have to deal with a larger passage of time and/or greater detail.

Focus on subject:

Descriptive Writing-requires you to closely observe a person, place, or thing. You are to learn it well enough that you can break it down into sections to discuss it. This form requires you to sue vivid sensory details and memory to bring the subject to life **and** clarify why the subject is important to you.

Eyewitness Account-shares the details of an event you witnessed, but the development is limited to that of a news story or report that includes the 5 W's and H (who?, what?, where?, when?, and how?).

Interview-primary source collection from a person whom you use to gather facts and details. In essay form, it is not acceptable to write the question and then provide the answer. The student must synthesize the material for the reader into a traditional five paragraph essay with thesis statement. In the interview essay it is often best to start with a description of the person being interviewed. The thesis will explain why you interviewed this person; it can appear in the beginning or at the conclusion.

Profile of a Person-in this form you are to research

the life of a person. The profile should cover a biographical story about the person, usually a special part of the person's life.

Historical Profile-a report about an interesting place in the past to bring the subject to life.

Venture Report-provides a detailed report about a specific occupation or business based upon the people who work in the industry.

Case Study-share the story of an individual whose experiences will speak for a larger group of people (people with disabilities, people who are bullied, survivors of a disaster).

I-Search Paper-presents your quest to find information about a subject of personal interest to you.

The Persuasive Essay.

The Persuasive essay explains why something is right or wrong based on personal opinion. It is often associated with the 'pet peeve.' Unless specifically requested to write this type of essay, do not do so. To have a 'pet peeve' in academia you must be writing from a position of authority. Have you been studying political science professionally for a number of years? If not, you are not an expert on the economy and cannot give imperative advice to the President. If you are told to write in this form, do not provide a rant. A rant is when the speaker only states their position and how stupid everyone else is for not having the same position. This position is not based on logical reasons explaining how and why the writer came to believe their position, which is what the persuasive essay should do. The danger with this essay is that no matter how it is phrased it is opinioned based. If your professor is a liberal democrat and you are a conservative republican, or the professor is an atheist and you are a Christian, the professor will punish you for expressing your opinion because in the world of academia, such positions as conservative and Christian are scientifically unfeasible and therefore should the student is incapable of scholarly reasoning. Beware!

The Process Essay.

The process essay, or how-to, arranges information by a significant pattern, either step-by-step so someone can produce a product or in sequence so the reader understands the process behind something.

The Comparison and Contrast Essay.

Both the compare, contrast, or a combined compare and contrast essays organize information into units of equal similarities or differences to present balanced information about each topic. These papers are often combined to show the writer knows how to shift between subjects as well. The most common problem with this essay is that students fail to follow their own established order for their information. Moreover, the assignment may be a trick. If the assignment states only contrast, any comparisons you make are digressions and unimportant points for your grade. Make sure you stay within the assignment by paying careful attention to the wording.

The Cause and Effect Essays.

The cause and effect essays present how something occurred or the reasons why something occurred. The most frequent difficulty for students is that they want to present a causal chain, in which one act leads to another to produce a third. (While historically it may be true that George W. Bush was elected president of

America, then terrorist attacks occurred in America, then war was declared on Iraq, it still would not that electing President Bush caused the war in Iraq, Historically many people were born the year of 9-11 but that does not mean their births caused the war. This is known as faulty logic, building a premise for the argument on facts that are not truly related.) Moreover, this assignment has the same dangers as the compare and contrast above. You must stick scrupulously to what is assigned. You cannot add effects to an assignment to write about the causes of a recent event. Mentioning one aspect of this group does not allow segue into the other.

The Definition Essay.

The definition essay explains an abstract term, something that is not physically present and cannot be touched (things like love, friendship, tact, patriotism). The purpose of this essay is to show you can think abstractly and critically by explaining your own definition. The major problem with this essay is that student writers often want rely on someone else's meaning and include dictionary definitions which present general thinking and ideas about the word being defined.

The Problem-Solution Essay.

The problem and solution essay is an examination of a problem from different angles and full discussion of possible solutions to eliminate the problem. The difficulty with this essay is that students pick topics that they have no background for, such as the current economic crisis or racism. Current topics are bad choices because you have to write what teacher's thinking. Unlike other combination essay assignments, like compare/contrast or cause/effect, this assignment leads from one to the other. Typically if you are asked to write about a problem, you are almost always, 99.9% of the time, expected to propose a solution as well, not just explain why a problem exists. This is the one area where even if it does not say write about a problem and solution, it is safe to do so.

The Research Paper.

The research paper, also known as the expository essay, this paper is a thesis statement plus support in which you inform readers about a subject without arguing for or against it or reflecting on its value and worth—that is weighing one side more than the other. The topic research should be divided equally among pro and con. This paper is considered impartial because equal time is devoted to contrasting voices about the topic. It may lay the ground work for an argument paper. The most frequent problem is presenting the topic in a limited focus. This paper is typically assigned as a preliminary method of learning the argument paper. It may also appear in upper-division classes in which you are only expected to survey theories and understand how these theories have changed over the course of scholarship on subjects relating to this discipline.

The Argument Paper.

The argument paper goes a step further than the research paper and presents your position on a subject by analysis of experts in the field. In this essay, think of yourself as an attorney. You need to present evidence that other intelligent people familiar with this subject believe the same things you do. The most frequent problem students have is that they do not present multiple examples and scholars who support their statements. For example, if I wanted to write a paper claiming students should be subjected to corporal punishment I could find someone who has been published somewhere who would agree in corporal punishment. I could even find them in scholarly journals. The problem is I would find few psychologists and sociologists who would advocate this as a primary method of correction for students in schools. Similarly, students do not explore which side of the debate is in favor; they only grab a source and put it in. Moreover, they do not check to see how much or where this person has published. A single source from a self-published person is not worth as much in academia as a person who has submitted their work for review at a university publishing house which requires at least four scholars in that field to read the work and approve the scholarship before it is printed by the publisher.

The Empirical Study.

The empirical study presents primary research as opposed to the above secondary research. The form presents a hypothesis and then explains how the hypothesis was tested and whether it was true, false, or invalid results. Unlike other papers this one will require an 'I' perspective for much of the writing since the writer must conduct some test or observation to prove the hypothesis. This paper still requires research. Writers must put their experiment into context with what others have performed and learned about the subject.

The Writing Process and You

Now that we have reviewed the types of academic writing you will be asked to do, we will discuss the process you will follow in this book.

An important distinction is made in this book between following a specific genre model, like a particular example in most composition guides, and following a general model or template, as a completed writing that was published and is considered an exemplum of writing. In the particular example of an already published piece of writing, that writer of the piece has found a pattern that worked for him or her — they are not still struggling to do so. It will not necessarily work for you and the content you want to talk about.

In contrast, following a template you insert key ideas at strategic locations where seasoned writers (your professors) will expect to see them. This will not mean that you will not have work to do. Writing requires thinking. Essay writing is the highest level cognitive skill available in academia. It shows both how you think and why you think it. Needless to say, a pattern or template cannot make up for a lack of understanding of the content. If you do not know what you want to say, no one can help you say it clearly.

Asking Questions.

That is why the first step of writing should be between you and your own mind. This step is often referred to as brainstorming, and it is best done with pen and paper (or word document). When you think of an idea to write about, first list all the things you know about it and questions that you want to know about it.

Do not do this step in your head. Unlike note paper or word document, there is no retrieving what you thought five days from now. As you progress in your academic career, you may work on papers over weeks or months. Therefore, it is necessary you be able to retrieve your information.

Moreover, as a tutor, students will often ask me, do I need a citation on that information. This simple step, documenting what you knew before you began researching, will answer your question. If you did not know it before, put a notation on it.

Also, this practice will help you later. Your goal as a student is to become able to answer your own questions, that is to become a critical thinker. As you make a habit of writing down your questions, your brain will train itself to become a critical thinker—one that can recognize when it does not know the answer to something and hint to you to start researching to find the answer for yourself.

Asking the Right Questions.

Now that you know what you know and do not know the process most likely will lead you in the direction of what to look for. No matter how much you know about a subject you should not be writing from your own personal experiences. Academic writing is about learning from others, hence you will need some sources to support your claim.

This means locating, reading, and analyzing literature about your particular subject before anything can and should be written on your draft. Collectively, in rhetoric studies and composition, this is referred to as the writing process.

The Traditional Writing Process.

You will notice there is very little about how to do the actual writing: such as how and why you would choose one genre over another, how to mix genres, or how think in writing patterns. These guides will add the stages of planning, organizing, drafting, editing, and redrafting as things you must do to have a good paper, but not how to set about making the choices you have available to you as a conscious decision.

More specifically, the general process involves defining a topic and selecting sources for the paper (planning), analyzing, evaluating, and synthesizing the sources (organizing), writing the paper (drafting), checking the draft (editing), and possibly rewriting, if allowed (reorganizing). While this model works for a one-size-fits-all model, it can be tailored more to academic writing; this book follows a different process, which is developed below.

Write for a Specific Purpose.

Once you know what you know about a subject, and have an idea of all the things you still need to learn, you need to understand why you are writing about the subject. This does not mean why the teacher assigned it or what grade you want.

When I ask students why they are writing about a subject, the most common answer I receive is because they want a grade or because a writing assignment was required. It does not matter if the students chooses their own subject they still make the same answers. And the answer is wrong. Your writing should be based on your having learned something in your research about your topic which you want to communicate in written form.

Scholarly papers (academic) have only three reasons for existing: 1) they provide recent information about scholarly activity surrounding a subject, 2) they provide new information about the topic that has never been considered before, and/or 3) they present an informed person's reasons for choosing sides in a scholarly debate about the subject. Notice the three reasons do not have to mutually exclusive. It does not mean that you must have only one reason for writing, but you must have one of the three reasons to be in the game.

Of the three reasons, number one is the most common form a student will encounter. After all it takes many years of research to know what other people have not done. However, number one is also the weakest position. If you are just providing a list of other people's thoughts, you are not showing you know how to think yourself.

Planning to Write.

The two tasks in planning to write are defining your topic to a limited scope and finding research. These steps are connected; how you limit the topic will determine what scholarly works you need to find. The best research is that done by experts in the field. This will not include open access websites.

Students often tell me, but I do not know who the scholars of this field are. If you do not know, find out first. Look for articles that review the literature in the field in scholarly journals. Also, look at your textbooks, particularly textbooks for classes in your field that overview different subjects in that field. Typically, these classes will provide textbooks with scholars quoted, and it is a good bet that these scholars are respected in their field for an academic publishing house to publish the textbook.

Also, check the back of these books. Some introductions to fields will provide a list of "critical essays" you should read on the topic; these will have been written by experts in the field. For instance, in English the *Norton Anthology of Literature* provides a list of critical essays for every author listed in their collection. Smart English majors begin their research with these works and build on them with other writers on the topic of more recent origin.

Some fields will have reference books that will tell you who the noted authorities are on a subject. Again, in the English field, there are reference books on Contemporary Writers, Women Writers, etc. These collections have a brief overview of the literature written about an author's work until the date the collection was published. It also lists what is considered the best research on this particular writer.

Organizing Your Thoughts.

Having completed your research, you need a pattern to follow to emphasize what you have learned. To do that you will need to think about the genres above. Can you use just one to effectively present your information?

Sometimes the answer will be yes, but most frequently it will be no.

Either way, you need to consider the form. This is where templates will help you. If one pattern will work, just rewrite the templates to fit your situation and just fill them in. If you need more than one, start with a simple outline.

Outlining does not have to be hard, so don't cringe. Outlining is simply a notational device to keep you from digressing, and it comes in many forms.

Of primary importance is your thesis statement (the main point you want your reader to know). This should be limited to one sentence for a five paper or smaller essay and two sentences for six to twenty pages. The reason being is that if you cannot state what point you are making you will digress in your paper because you do not really know what point you are making.

It can be fine to be fuzzy about what you what the reader to know if you have plenty of time. Because without a solid point you want to make, you will have to do heavy editing to ensure you have not digressed in the paper after it is written.

And this step can be difficult for some students who love their own writing. Some students will not want to see any of their words cut once they have written them because they have written them. When I was a journalist on the student paper in high school, I felt the same way. I hated to see anything chopped from what I had produced because I had invested time and effort into what I put on the paper. At that time I had to write with an electric typewriter (yes, computers had been invented, but I didn't have access to one.), and writing required retyping everything anytime something was changed. When I felt I had gotten it perfect, I objected to other changing it.

Still, the journalist's pyramid writing was one of the best things I ever learned. The first sentence has to include as many of the who, what, where, when, and hows as possible, preferably in one sentence. The rest of the information is the hows and whys. Every sentence has to be constructed so that the last one can be removed, like a Russian nested doll, with the least information lost. The reason being that you are given a word count for your space, but news changes. Some other piece of information may need to be inserted. If you want your by-line in the paper somewhere, your writing has to be instantaneously edit-able. I worked at this writing because I loved to see my name in print. And, I learned writing never has a final form.

Like the journalist's pyramid, once you know what you want to say, you need to outline how you want to say it in a notation form. This way you include all the necessary information and avoid some of the mandatory cuts that will appear in free-flow writing.

Personally, I like brief references that keep me on track but do not fuss.

My Outline for This Book

Introduction-reason and purpose of book

Chapter One-overview of academic writing for students

    I.   Types of genres considered academic writing

    II.   The writing process

Notice in the box above, the outline does not cover all of the sub-headings I added to each section of these two chapters. In the first section, the Introduction, I only noted that I wanted to focus on why I was writing the book by presenting my reasons for writing the book and the purpose (how it differs from other writing guides someone might purchase:

- I did not present the information in complete sentences.
- I did not subdivide my points.
- I did not add my transitions between my points.

- I did not present my thesis for the overall book or for each chapter.

I could have done all of these things. All of these things would have eliminated editing time later.

However, when I write I like the sense of exploration of ideas as I see words appear. This means my writing style is never going to meticulously follow the outline after I have written it. Therefore, I will have to do heavy editing after my writing is complete in order to remove digressions from the work. Still, I like to digress. Those stories can often be cut and pasted as examples elsewhere or simply added to my journal.

The point is there is really no right or wrong way to do an outline, despite what teachers' tell you, unless it is a formal outline for publication. What you need is a road map. The more you can fill in the more guideposts you will have in writing the paper, but completing the road map should never inhibit your writing. If you obsess over the niggled details, you will only develop writer's block and hate writing.

As you get used to a simple outline, you should work on finding out how much detail you can produced in notation form before you are wasting time. Some people can compose a detailed outline. Write their thesis statement. Write all their main points. Write all their sub-points. Write all their examples and illustrations for their sub-points and note where each piece of scholarship will reinforce their points. Often they will write in complete sentences and add their transitions between their major and minor points. By sticking to this outline, they will produce a tight essay. They will have little revision to do because they have already eliminated digressions or unwanted material in the outline. They have already played with their pattern while their essay is still in its bare-bones state. Hence, it is easier for them to see where they have not provided adequate examples or support and where their essay may not present a logical argument. They do not see their essay as a body of words; they see it as a skeleton.

Anyone can learn to see this way. You only have to learn not to fear the outline.

The Zero-Draft.

Once you know what main point you want to make and have some general ideas about how to present it, you will begin the zero-draft. The zero-draft is the process of getting something, anything, down on paper. This is when you go from the blinking cursor on the screen to re-writing things to make them sound better.

The zero-draft is an important stage. Personally, I advise against working with a tutor or showing an instructor anything during this stage. While you are composing the zero-draft you are working out your argument and presentation of your ideas. You may not have fully formed what you want to say. If you show a tutor or teacher your work at this stage, they will make assumptions about where you want the work to go or how to get there. It will no longer be yours.

As a teacher with over ten years experience with writing students, you will be happier with advice that comes after you have completed the zero-draft. Never ask advice about what is in your head. Often you will change expression between verbally communicating what you want to say and writing it down. Remember, opinions can change with those expressions as well.

The best way to write the zero-draft is to just write.

- Do not worry about how you are phrasing information.
- Do not worry about contractions or pronoun usage.
- Do not worry if you start digressing.
- Write quickly.
- Do not edit grammar as you go.
- Do not worry if you have all your illustrations and examples included.

In short, do not worry. This is one reason you should never show your work to tutors or teachers during this stage. Tutors and teachers worry and fuss over syntax and grammar. They will point out errors. You will start focusing on those insignificant things and stop focusing on the content of what you are trying to say. If you have nothing important to say, it does not matter how grammatically correct it is or how well the syntax flows.

While you do not want to obsess on form at this point, it is best to start with a template and plug information in. In this way you will be working towards your final essay.

Unlike journal writing in which you just keep writing your thoughts that will have no place in your final product, template writing starts with the main ideas and getting them down in sections. By focusing on sections, you save the difficult parts, like a catchy hook and transitions, until the end of the essay. As you fill in the template sections and your mind is working on solving the problem of the writing assignment, you may realize this part of the template needs to move. Having it in pieces, it will be easier to do so. Imagine your writing as a bunch of blocks lying around. Each block is a unit of your information or argument. You can put them in any order; however, if you want a pattern to emerge, you will have to create it. The blocks can be ordered by colors, by pictures, by alphabet letters. Any of these things or a combination of them on the blocks can be used to create an overall design. For instance, you could spell out the words 'way to go' bordered with red blocks, bordered with blue blocks.

On the other hand, they could appear haphazard as well with no obvious attempt at arranging the information. Students often present this method when they submit an unrevised essay using the traditional essay writing model, with students writing their hook, thesis, first paragraph, second paragraph, third paragraph, and conclusion. Voila!

Unhappily, the result is often not voila. Some students never take time to think about where these blocks of information would appear to their best advantage because they do not think of them as blocks of information, and they do not want to break the flow of their words.

Writing in units you do not break the flow of the words because it is created within the sections themselves. You will then build the frame around them with topic sentences, transitions, and concluding sentences once you have the blocks in the correct order for your purposes.

Revising.

Using the template method, you are revising less for flow and more for content which has a higher impact on the final grade of a paper.

Yes, you will still have to revise. As you are plugging in information into the block, if you realize that you need more information about that section, you will research and add it.

You will not be endlessly researching to no specific purpose. Once you have your background, all of your writing time will be working for a reason — to prove or disprove a thesis.

The reason for revising is to create the biggest impact with your words. You do that in blocks by arranging them and ensuring you have supports and examples.

Editing.

This is the stage most students call revising. If they change a comma, they insist they have revised. However, this is editing. Once you have your skeleton constructed in the revision stage by playing with your blocks of information, you will be ready to move on to the true editing stage.

Re-reading each page sentence by sentence for syntax and mechanical errors; this means reading for sentences that make no sense alone and for those pesky grammar errors. The best way to complete this stage is to start at the back of your paper. Read the last sentence you wrote. Does it make sense?

If it does not, revise it. If it does, move on to the sentence before it. Keep going until you arrive at the first sentence of the essay.

Often students will include fragments or partial sentences because we talk that way. They can be difficult for students to recognize when reading a paper straight through from beginning to end. Sadly, the fragment will typically be part of the sentence in front of it or behind it. Therefore, reading the paper quickly, it will join up with the information it belongs within the writer's mind.

The best way to identify fragments is to read each sentence out of context by reading backwards. The writer's mind will say, whoa there, something is wrong here.

These last two stages in the writing process are interactive, meaning that you will probably be shifting between them as you write. It is difficult to keep revising and editing distinctly separate activities because if you misspell a word your impulse is to go back and change it while you know where it is. Also, while you are checking to see if you included your examples and transitions, you will notice grammar errors, and the same is true in the editing stage. While you are ruthlessly eliminating grammar errors, you may think of another point that would help your essay, which means more writing if you want that A.

It is not uncommon for professional writers to rewrite three or more drafts, each time thinking they are finishing the piece. Good writing takes time and effort. It also takes thought and thinking is hard work. Plan for it.

A Last Word about Practically Stress-free Writing

While you should not worry if it takes you multiple drafts to get the grade you want, you should not force your writing either—it leads to writer's block. To write without stress is probably unrealistic while you are in school, but there are things you can do to reduce the stress.

- At the beginning of the semester find out what writing assignments are required for the class. Find out the due dates and write them in a calendar. Block that day off—you will have finished product before that!
- Now, you have from the beginning of class until the day before the paper is due or from the time of the due date of the previous assignment until the next due date.
- Do this with all of your classes written assignments, using different colored inks for your different classes. You will notice this shortens the available time considerably, right here.
- Count the days for each paper. Do not count holidays. These are meant to refresh you by not working. Factor in your work schedule if you have a job.

- Make a schedule for each paper; if essays overlap put the schedules side-by-side. It might look something like the table given below.

Producing practically stress-free writing is more about knowing what you want to say and how to go about saying it than anything else. Some students interpret this as, "when I have an idea, I don't have to worry about the paper until when it is due." Some will insist they are working on their writing because they are thinking about it in their mind. Days later when it comes to actually putting the words down paper they do not remember how they wanted to phrase things or which topics they knew they must include. They have envisioned a beautiful paper in their dreams. It is not a reality. The teacher can only grade what is really there in black and white on their paper.

I won't say it cannot be done to think out a paper and write it out the day it is due. I have seen it done by only two people with any type of success. I was a student for twenty-two years, a tutor and teacher for ten years. As both student and teacher, I saw many students who claimed they could whip out an A paper using this method, but they could not.

I firmly believe it is best to use notes and work on the essay in pieces, planning to revise for flow and structure later. There is less stress to editing a paper that is in page requirement length than to produce one from scratch. Organizing the pieces I only have to determine how to arrange my information as I have already produced a thesis and topic sentences. I may need to change them to make them flow better, but I don't have to worry about what topics to discuss. I also do not have to worry about a perfect quote coming to mind but not remembering which source it was in. Not to mention finding one topic I had planned to write about was really a subtopic of another, meaning I need to find another point to prove my argument. Now, I have more research to do and the paper is due in what??, fifteen minutes. OMG!

Practically stress-free writing is accomplished just by planning. Establishing some topics, doing the research for them, writing a paragraph using the sources. Jotting down a great inspiration for an opening hook. Explaining the 'so what' of your paper in detail, which will later migrate to your conclusion. It is getting the pieces done that matters.

Once you know how to work with pieces rather than an essay, you will also know how to grow a paper, to build on it for another assignment. While college classes do not allow you to resubmit papers (you can be expelled for that), you can rework papers by adding new topics—comparing one thing to another, changing focus to explain why something occurred, etc. In this manner you can use your sources over and over again, as long as they are still current.

Finding ways to overlap research assignments can save you time and effort. Professional writers do this all the time. A writer may research Paul Revere for a piece to be sold in a school magazine. The same research may be converted into a short play to be sold, or a short story. Information is recycled into other forms. This method will come in handy if you plan to go on to graduate school.

To start with, however, focus on charting your work. This will give you information about how you write, when you write, and how long it takes you to write. Novice writers under- and over-estimate how long writing takes for them. They expect someone familiar with writing to be able to tell them how long they will need, but no one can do this.

Writing is a personal experience. Each step takes you as long as it takes you. You will find as you keep track of your progress that you will learn ways to take time off writing. You will learn what areas you can push through quickly and which you cannot rush.

For me, I can do my research quickly. I have learned to use databases efficiently, more efficiently than other students. If I am pressed for time, I can eliminate it here. Generally, I like to spend time researching and reading new articles, but it is not necessary to my grade. What I cannot rush is editing. I must finish my paper in advance of the due date. I must have time to set it aside, to disconnect from it, even if it is only a little bit. If I do not have this time, I will have sentences that do not make sense because I have left words out, and I will have grammar errors because I focus on getting the general concepts down, not whether or not a comma is mandatory.

In order to learn what steps you need to follow you should start with a chart like the one below.

Time	Activity	Goal	Accomplished
9-10	Write two annotated bibliographies	Write 200-300 words for each bibliography	586 words
10-11	Write paragraph on topic X using sources	Write 500 words	514
11-12	Write background review for intro	Write 250 words	276
12-1	LUNCK BREAK		
1-2	Write theses	Write 30 words	25
2-3	Write paragraph on topic XX using sources	Write 500 words	
3-4	Read over paragraphs written		

Notice, here that the activity is separated from the goal. You need both a purpose and an aim. From 9-10 am, the purpose is to read two articles and write two annotated bibliographies in that slotted time. To complete this activity, the student would also have to write two annotated entries between 200 and 300 words, or a total of 400 to 600 words. In the accomplished box, I put the student on a morning roll. The student completed the readings and wrote both entries for a combined total of 586 words on paper.

From 10-11 the student remained on a roll. They wrote the paragraph that will appear in their essay using these two sources. The anticipated word count on the paragraph was 500 words; the student completed it in 514. After adding these sources, the student then moved on to less critical examination. The student began drafting an introductory paragraph based on explaining background about the topic. Since an introductory paragraph should be about a third to a half a page, the student anticipated a 250 word count on the introduction. In the Accomplished box, the student noted that they went over the anticipated count.

After this busy morning, the student planned the lunch break. Taking a whole hour to eat and relax.

When the student returned to work at 1, the student planned something not writing intensive, but thought intensive—the crafting of a thesis statement. Although the student wanted the thesis to only be one long sentence (30 words), the student allowed an entire hour to working on this most important point of the paper. Noted in the Accomplished box is the current thesis was completed in 25 words, under the expected limit.

From 2-3 the student wrote another body paragraph for the paper, or plans to as the chart is not filled in yet.

Notice the last entry from 3-4. This time is used to review what has been done during the day. The student is working on revision, checking the patter and arrangement of what has been said in the paragraphs and checking it against the annotated bibliography and source article. It is not a time to write more on different topics. The student is spending the time organizing what they will write during their next session based on what they have accomplished in this one.

Tips

- ❖ When making your own writing schedule, be sure to leave space for both the activity and your progress on it.
- ❖ If you have several days with large blocks of time available for writing, you may want to make two charts: one with the overall progress before the due date and one with detailed hourly plans of activities and expected word counts.
- ❖ Plan time for recreation as well as work.
- ❖ Be aware that working to schedules takes time to get used to. No one is clocking you in and checking on you. You must learn to manage yourself.

Essay for English (Due in one week) and History (due in a week and a half)				
Days of the Week	Activity for English Paper	Finished or Not	Activity for History Paper	Finished or Not
Mon	Decide on topic: book and thesis statement		Decide on topic: Thesis statement	
Tues	Background and research / Work 6-10		Background and research /Work 6-10	
Wed	Simple outline: start working on template sections /Work 6-10		Simple outline/ Work 6-10	
Thurs	Template sections: zero draft			

Friday	Zero-draft		Template Sections: Zero draft	
Sat.	Revising		Zero-draft	
Sun.	Editing		Zero-draft	
Mon.	Paper Due Today!!!!		Revising	
Tues			Editing	
Weds.			Paper Due Today!!!!	

You need have this chart in a place where you can see it. If you keep reminding yourself you have work to do, you will do it. The sections can be arranged in parts too. For instance, you can put a research day. Write thesis, Work on point one. Next day, work on point two. How much you want to accomplish each day is up to you and the day your paper is due.

Remember a steady progress towards your goal is better than a mad-cap rush to finish.

If you have to write two papers in the same time frame, try to organize them together. More importantly, try to overlap topics. In this case if I have chosen my classes well I can write a history paper on the English stage during the reign of Queen Elizabeth and a literature paper on Christopher Marlowe, who wrote plays during this period. I can use Marlowe as an example in my history paper, and I can use the history of the English stage as background in my literature paper.

Try to make nothing mutually exclusive. It is more work with less profit. Even if you get an A on both papers, you do not get more of an A because you worked harder instead of smarter.

Also try to keep all your research time together. One day doing library research for both papers. Then outline both papers so you remember where you were going with your research.

Nevertheless, only write one paper at zero-draft at a time. Until you have finished the zero-draft of the one do not start the other. Otherwise, sources and information will start blurring together and your information will reflect it in your writing.

Do not worry about completely finishing everything on that day. Just note it and move it down. The idea of the schedule is to have you doing a little so it does not matter if something comes up to put your schedule off.

While it may not seem like much of a writing difference, this is a big difference. The one-shot overnight essay can be derailed by suddenly finding you have to work longer than expect, being involved in a car accident on the way home, catching the flu, your computer dropping and breaking, or even finding you are not in the mood to write. I don't care attitudes come through loud and clear in your writing.

The physical act of setting aside time for the writing will help you place it as a priority and it will also help you learn how you write   so that these chunks of time will be more and more effectively used as you learn how you need to focus while you are writing.

No guide to writing can tell you what writing process will work best for you. The more you are aware of how and when you write most effectively, the better you will be able to consciously incorporate that information into planning how produce an A paper every time, no matter what.

For Teachers

There are several things you can do to improve students' ability to write in an academic voice:

- Explain to students why they need to master this form of writing; how it differs from a creative voice, like poetry.
- Have students write in different voices as a contrast—to show they can use different styles just as they do vocally by singing and talking.
- Allow students to help prepare a rubric for grading as a class. Start by identifying what they like about certain passages provided to them written by A-level writers.
- Help students understand where their writing process is. They may not know they have only used brainstorming and drafting until the write a narrative about the steps they follow to complete a paper.
- Show students how to make a table and keep track of their writing time. Give them points for doing so.

Things that are not graded seem to have no value to students. Reinforce the importance of these steps by assigning them points that are incorporated into the final grading of the paper.

Having students work on the paper in pieces ensures they can complete each step in producing a quality paper, that they do not skip over steps and thereby learn to 'slap' a paper together overnight, and that they do not plagiarize. Students who have been closely monitored through the writing process cannot purchase or download papers to try and fit them to your assignments. Since plagiarized papers do not come in pieces, students would lose substantial points by not showing work as it is completed, negating the benefits of plagiarizing.

Chapter 2

Template for Creating the Standard Academic Paper

The following guide will help you organize the core parts of your essay, and it will help you learn to see the outline necessary to produce a quality essay. (All of final essay should be double spaced throughout, including contact information and works cited paged.)

Creating an academic essay is partly a matter of filling in information at expected places in the essay. A brilliant essay is not about reinventing the writing wheel, but using it to stress information and make your points easier for the reader to follow along. This matter is largely a matter of form. That does not mean your essay need not be brilliant. It does mean that your brilliance shows in how you think about your topic and what you have to say about your topic, not the way in which you say it.

Because students only have to write one or two essays in any given genre of writing, students often fail to learn how to recognize those patterns in more complex pieces of writing like the standard academic paper which is a mixed genre piece. Because information needs to be plugged into the essay at selected points it is possible to reduce the standard academic essay to a template in order for you to produce a zero draft paper in a way that will put the pieces into their required slots, saving you time later as you polish your writing.

Although the parts of the template follow the outline of a finished paper, you do not need to begin working on inserting the information in any particular order. Some students like to save things like the introductory hook until last as they know that their writing will take a firmer shape and viewpoint as they work on refining and polishing their writing. It would, therefore, be a waste of time for those students to sit down, craft and polish a perfect hook for an early draft that would have no bearing on the final piece of writing.

*   *   *   *   *   *   *   *   *

Essay Template

[GO TO INSERT AND PUT A HEADER & FOOTER WITH LAST NAME AND PAGE NUMBER]

Every paper needs a standard form of reference for noting your first and last name, the you are submitting the paper for, the instructor's name teaching the course, and the date.

It seems to come as a surprise to some students but they do not have a monopoly on their name. Others, not related to them may bear the same name. Occasionally, it even happens in the same class. More commonly, it happens that a teacher will have two students with same name in different classes. This is why a student should always put their first and last name on their work.

The teacher's name and course should appear in case the papers are left somewhere by either the teacher or student. This information allows the paper to find its way home.

Let's start at the beginning. Every essay should have what is called a header. A header on an essay is not the same thing as a header in a Microsoft Word Document. In the Word Document a header refers to a part of the page layout design, a section or strip of blank space usually left at the top margin of a document. By clicking on the header in the Word Document a person can add information to the area that is usually left as white space. This is not what is meant by a header on an essay. A header, for an essay, is a collection of precise information about the writer and publication of the essay. In MLA format it includes only the author of the essay's first and last name, the complete title of the course for which the paper is being written as a partial fulfillment of the course requirements, the name of the instructor who will grade the essay, and the date the essay is due to show which term the paper is submitted for in case the instructor keeps copies on file for other students to examine.

Section 1: The Header.

This information should appear in the top left hand of the first page:

First name Last name

Course

Instructor's name

Date

This information should not appear in the page design header of the Word program, as stated above. It should start inside the normal space for writing on a blank Microsoft Word document. An example is given in the picture below.

Figure 1 Illustration of proper place for essay header.

As opposed to:

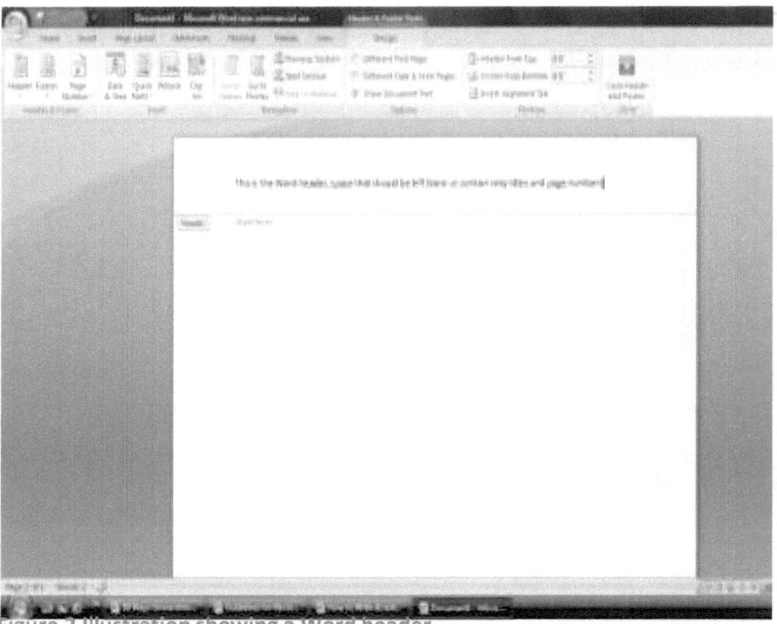

Figure 2 Illustration showing a Word header.

The header of a student paper is for bookkeeping purposes. You will want a grade for your work. This information ensures the teacher knows who to credit.

Although the date may not seem important, it may determine whether or not the work is graded. Teachers who do not accept late papers may not accept a paper that is left for them without proper dating and cataloging at the department mailroom.

- ✓ Including the date is more important for the student than the teacher. Instead of putting the date of the day you begin writing the paper, put the due date of the essay. Then you will have a constant reminder of when the paper is to be turned in.
- ✓ Always include automatic page numbering on your essays as well. I once turned in a paper and received a low grade on it. A large question mark appeared on the second page. I had mis-ordered the unnumbered pages of the essay to 1,3,2,4. Before I left class, I showed the instructor what had happened and he graciously agreed to re-examine my grade. In the order I gave him, my argument made no sense. If I had put the numbers on the essay, he could have seen for himself that the pages were simply out of order. After this incident I always double checked that I had included page numbers on my essay.

Differences in formatting styles between MLA, Chicago Manual of Style, APA, and others, vary in where this personal information should appear. Follow the guide your teacher tells you to. Some styles, like APA, will require a cover page for the information. Others, like MLA, will include the information on the first page of the essay. Some styles require additional information.

Sloppy arrangement of your discipline's style information or missing information will present you as a careless writer. If an instructor goes into grading the paper thinking you are careless, they will be more attune to looking for errors in your work.

- ✓ Make sure you have provided only the information required.
- ✓ Make sure all the required information is present.

Section 2: The Title, or Grabbing the Reader.

Some students like to begin with a title and grow the paper from there. Others wait until the end to do this.

A title is not a label. A paper should never be submitted with a centered label 'Essay One.' A title is the first bit of information that can make a reader want to reader your work. In this case, make your instructor want to read what you have written.

Many was the time I took all the essays with labels and put them at the bottom of my reading stack. They are a chore to read. Yes, I was being paid to read them, but that doesn't mean I enjoyed them. At least students who came up with titles were trying to capture my attention and make the duty less painful.

An appropriate title is often an indication of the student's creativity. If the student has come up with an intriguing title, usually their work is better written, well developed, and well reasoned.

What is Your Title?

A title is not the same thing as a label. The title must reflect the context of your specific essay.
(This piece has a label because it is a form, not an essay.) Therefore, the title 'Essay' will not work unless you are writing about how to write an essay. Moreover, the title should reflect something about your attitude towards your subject. Hence, the title 'Drug Abuse' is no good either.

You can use a question *if*, and only if, your entire paper is answering that specific question. So, you could have as an appropriate title 'Why Do Teenagers Abuse Prescription Drugs?', but the paper must be answering only this question. The minute you start talking about the warning signs of drug abuse or what to do about drug abuse, your title no longer fits your paper.

When you are coming up with your title, think about what your paper is trying to accomplish.

- A Response to Alice Walker's *The Color Purple*
  - This title implies a first person discussion of things the reader connected with in the text.
- A Fresh Look at Civil Rights
  - This title implies the paper will not be discussing Susan B. Anthony, Martin Luther King, or even the Rev. Jesse Jackson's role in furthering minorities. It would be expected to explain where San Antonio, Texas (insert your city), or America stands (within the last five years) on promoting racial equality.
- Two Cheers for Education
  - This title implies that education needs improving based on the English phrase, "Three cheers for so and so: Hip, Hip, Hurray!"

As a working title for your draft, you may start with just a topic, like Education, until you are sure how you will approach the topic, but it should never appear on an instructor's desk in that form.

The title is one of two opportunities you as a writer have to get the reader interested in what you have to say. Many students undervalue the importance of making their writing pleasurable for the reader. Hopefully, this will change with the new y-generation and its fascination with facebook, twitter, and blogs. Readers seldom stay with writers who cannot capture their interest, there are too many other things to do. It is imperative that opportunities to interest the reader are used to their full advantage.

Section 3: Grabbing the Reader, Part Two.

The second opportunity to get the reader's attention is the opening of your writing. This is called the hook. A hook needs to utilize the reader's desire for information that is relevant to his or her situation or status. People like to read things that make them informed, that help them understand a situation, person, or cause. The job of the hook is to make information seem relevant to the reader — to give them a reason to keep reading.

A hook can come in many forms.

The Hook

Outside of class people are not paid to read your writing. It is your job as the writer to grab the attention of the reader in order to get your message across.

This is also a task that is often best left until after you have completed the zero (from nothing to something) draft of the essay.

Typical hooks include

- a startling fact
  - Did you know that America generates more than 34 tons of food waste per year? (culinate.com).
- a story
- an example
- a brief history of the topic
- your definition for an abstract concept (like *love* or *patriotism*); do not provide a definition that can be found in a dictionary, unless you need to show you have mastered terms for class (like, Shakespeare's poem is a sonnet, fourteen lines of iambic pentameter that are rhymed in a specific pattern, focusing on a lover's sense of loss regarding the

beloved's absence.) To have an extended definition you must provide more than what everyone else thinks: i.e. Patriotism is more that joining a branch of the armed forces or flag flying on the fourth of July while fireworks explode. Patriotism is . . . . [Notice I did not include a statement like "There are many definitions of patriotism." Unless your audience is stupid there is no reason to do so.]

Write your hook:

_____

_____

_____

_____

_____

_____

Your hook should never be a generality:

* ❖ War is horrible.
* ❖ Education is important in America.
* ❖ There are many different cultures in American society.

❖ People died from many different causes.

The reason students include statements of this type varies. Some students need anything down on paper or on the screen in order to get to their problem, which is not a problem unless it stays in the essay.

Others misunderstand the advice to start with the topic in a general manner and narrow down to the thesis statement. They believe that this means if they want to talk about the second Iraqi War that they should being with the general aspects of war; however, this is not the case. These students need to start with the general background of the Iraqi War, then narrow to their specific point about this particular war. General statements like war is horrible are fillers — statements that do not advance an argument. They rely on commonplaces and general assumptions made by cultures. Good essays are not are not about making general assumptions or finding your place within the cultural norms surrounding you. Good essays are about finding your own voice and displaying your interests in an appropriate manner — this cannot be done if you insert other people's clichés, proverbs, and general assumptions about life.

A more interesting way to engage the reader is to inform them how many American lives were lost in the conflict or how many people volunteered to serve within the first month after the 9-11 Twin Towers bombing. In other words, tell them something they are unlike to know, not what they do know.

Section 4: The General Introduction Body.

The Introduction

Your introduction will appear between the Hook and the Thesis. It **must** provide a link to the thesis, but it can do more. This is the section where you need to give background about your topic, explain definitions, or other things that your reader will need to know in order to understand your essay.

For my example on education, I might move from a hook (How many American students are failed by our compulsory education each year?
The introduction would establish that there is a problem. X number of white students fail; Y number of black students fail; Z number of Hispanic students fail.

I could further my problem by adding a narrative about a recently graduated high school student, named B, who cannot find employment because, although she graduated, she lacks adequate skills to perform entry level work and will have to take developmental, for which the government does not pay, classes in order to be able to enter the local junior college .

Then I need to transition to my thesis: Students are unprepared for life and higher education because the American education system is not adequate to meet t o day' s needs.

Then I can add my thesis.

(An introduction is typically one-third of a page-- total.)

Write your introduction:

_____

_____

_____

_____

_____

Section 5: The Transition.

The transition is a sentence that connects the ideas from your hook to your thesis statement. If, for example, you told a story about seeing a homeless person huddled in a doorway rather than seeking shelter, you would need to bridge this description with a statement about what your paper will explore: *Today's society tries to eliminate homelessness without understanding how its various root causes impact the psychological development of human beings.*

Students will often want to jump from the story to their point.

A good introduction will explain the connection with a statement like — *Although this is only one experience, understanding human responses to different situations is an important aspect of understanding homelessness.*

This sentence has two necessary parts:

[Connection to the previous story (not given here)] and connection to central topic psychological development.

Let's look at the sentence again by parts:

[Although this is only one experience,]

This part above is the reference to the story the reader would have just finished, telling the reader there is more to this story than just an interesting vignette of American society. This part of the connection is written in a dependent clause—a clause that cannot stand alone as a complete sentence—to show that this story is not the main focus or point of the person's writing. That is, the writer has another, greater goal in mind.

The sentence continues with a independent clause—one that can stand alone:

understanding human responses to different situations is an important aspect of understanding homelessness.

This portion helps the reader transition to homelessness being part of an individual's response to a set of circumstances that he or she has experienced. This sentence helps readers narrow their expectations from the many things your vignette could be leading towards to understanding human responses to the events that shape our lives.

Section 6: The Thesis.

Every piece of writing needs an aim and purpose. Most writing guides refer to this aim and purpose as a thesis statement. It is the core of a piece of writing. It acts as a skeletal frame upon which you place you arguments and introduce your facts to support this core idea.

WARNING. Although this part of your introduction demands a thesis statement, remember you do not have to write your paper in any particular order. You could start with body paragraphs, or even your conclusion. However, when you order your paper, you must put the parts in the proper order. So, although you do not have to write down the template, you will be able to insert your parts into the proper template frame.

Imagine your body without your bones — your arms would just be lumps of flesh and muscles that would be difficult to coordinate and use. While it would be possible to get along without a few of your bones, your body would not be able to function without any of them. Moreover, if some bones, like your rib cage, were to disappear, you would be venerable. You would not be able to lead the life you do now, certainly, but more than that you would have to ensure that you were never bumped or jostled if you wanted to keep your heart going.

The thesis acts in much the same way as your heart for a piece of writing – it protects you main idea and keeps it alive and free from harm. However, if you fail to add the bones to protect the idea, the heart, or thesis, can end up lost within the lump of flesh. It cannot protect itself for attacks, or people who may disagree with your thesis. Indeed, it may not even be able to function efficiently to keep you alive as it may be weighted down by other less significant things.

However, to have any life at all, your piece of writing requires that there be heart in it. Moreover, this heart needs to be small.

Your heart cannot be the size of your body – it just would not function efficiently. Well, your thesis needs to have this same rule applied to it. Like your heart that supports something bigger, your thesis supports your larger paper.

As a general guide, keep this in mind:

A good thesis

> For works 5 pages or under
→   one sentence
> For works between 20 pages and 5 pages
→   two sentences

For works between 50 pages and 21 pages
→   three sentences
For works over 50 pages
→   four sentences

and these are outside limits, meaning you cannot exceed them or go beyond them in any form or fashion, except under exceptional circumstances!

The reason the requirement is so small is that the thesis reflects your ability as a writer to think clearly. Mores sentences typically reflect a writer's inability to focus and clearly state what he or she wants to say.

If you think you cannot reduce your thesis to one sentence, just get a digital recorder and ask a friend to listen to you explain the importance of your paper. At some point as you talk to your friend, you will reduce the importance to just one sentence.

When I tutor I hear students say all the time that their point cannot be written in just one sentence. Yet when I ask them to start talking about their paper and why it is important, what they want the reader to take away from their piece of writing, they automatically reduce the paper into exactly what they need in the paper — a one sentence summary of everything they want to say. Many of them will recognize what they have just done. Unfortunately, fear of writing also means that they frequently have immediate amnesia and cannot restate it. That is why it is helpful, not just to have a friend present, but a digital recorder going. When you have actually got to the point that you have your main point in one sentence, you just have to listen to it again and type it out. If you rely just on a friend you may find that they were napping at the critical juncture or are so excited for you that they are unable to recall exactly what you said either.

Although the thesis or main point belongs in this spot for your paper, you do not have to have a rock solid thesis to write your first draft.

Never obsess over any point of writing.

A) It does not good.
B) Writing is not engraved in stone; it can always be changed later.

The Thesis

This is the main point you want your reader to know about your subject. It should include both the topic (*education*) **and** an attitude towards the subject (*in America is in dire straits*) **and** reason(s) (*because of the focus on "No Child Left Behind," teaching certifications that require behavioral classes instead of competency in* *subjects other than sociology/psychology, and financial resources directed at administrators instead of teachers*).

This is a mini-blueprint of your entire essay. The essay would need *at least* one paragraph on each of the reasons listed. Each single paragraph may require five, it depends on how likely your audience is to assume your position is justifiable.

This is not your introduction!! A thesis may only be one or two sentences long, no matter if the entire essay is one page or six hundred.

There are two types of thesis statements — explicit and indirect.

Explicit: This type provides the reasons which will be developed in the body. Most teachers prefer the explicit method so they can follow along to see if you are digressing or failing to support your claims with proof. This method was used in the example above.

Indirect: This type of essay provides a general topic and attitude only. The indirect method type appears in longer works in which the conclusion will focus on recapping the entire argument, and it is generally used in arguments in which the writer knows the audience will resist the claim.

There is no such thing as an *implied thesis* where the audience has to guess your intentions. There is an unstated thesis option; however, if you cannot articulate your claim and reasons clearly, the paper will appear to have no direction (a grade of D or F), in contrast to a paper that fails to provide adequate proof (a grade of B or C).

To find your thesis provide the following information:

Your topic:

Your attitude towards your topic:

Reason #1 why your topic is true:

Reason #2 why your topic is true:

Reason #3 why your topic is true:

Reason #4 why your topic is true:

Reason #5 why your topic is true:

Reason #6 why your topic is true:

And so on! The number of reasons depends on the amount of things you have to say. You should always have at least two reasons to show that your ideas are not an anomaly — or something that exists as an exception to the rules. However, the actually number you need to include depends upon the strength of each reason to support your main point. The more points you have the less you need to worry about how strong your points are. You can convince by numbers as well as by strength of argument.

Now, place these pieces into a sentence:

_____

_____

_____

Some examples to fill in:

Topic G is important because (reason #1), (reason #2) , and (reason #3).

Example: [Understanding educational goals in America (Topic G)] is important because (the American economy has fallen into a decline shown by the current recession), (although many workers are unemployed businesses are still looking to hire foreign workers for the skills they require), and (educational systems continue to produce students trained for jobs in closed industries).

Although (reason #3) has been widely debated, (reason #1) and (reason #5) are more important to Topic Z.

Example: Although male students' ability to dominate class discussions and be perceived as student leaders has been widely debated, classroom dynamics and individual personality types are more important to understanding gendered behavior.

Find a couple of thesis statements that you like in your articles as you work on your research. Write them out and identify the topic, attitude, and reasons. Try substituting your own opinions in these forms. In fact, keep a list of these for future use. You are not stealing someone's idea or paper. You are modeling the form in which they constructed their ideas. The form is not their property. You must, however, be placing your own original content within the slots (as demonstrated above), not rewording their ideas.

Section 7: The Body.

Body Paragraph # 1

One claim, in a complete sentence, that supports your thesis—the topic sentence.

Ex. The American education system is suffering because of the bill known as "No Child Left Behind."

This claim cannot stand on its own; it must be proven. Since many legislators and teachers make this claim in this area, I would not need to provide as much documentation that this statement is believed, but I would have to prove many different groups are opposed to this bill.

Supporting Detail #1
This is a specific, concrete example. For example, I might use an article from the *New York Times* in which Senator so and so states that the "No Child Left Behind" policy is bad for American schools and give a quote from the article (followed by a citation). Followed by a comment on why this quote is important to understand that the American education system is suffering.

Sandwich Quote for all Supporting Detail:
1) Introduce source
2) Quote or summarize source
3) Citation
4) Explain why quote is important to thesis

All information from sources should appear in a Sandwich Quote. You must provide the credentials of your source. Imagine telling your friends that a paper is due next Friday. The information would be perceived based on your credibility. If you are a prankster, the people you tell would not trust you. The information would also be perceived differently if you do not know the people you tell. Even if you are not a prankster, they may not believe you. So to, it would be interpreted differently if you stated, 'Mr. Black, our English teacher, said the paper is due on next Friday.' Mr. Black has more authority because he grades the paper. If you said, 'my friend, John, said the paper is due on Friday next,' the audience would have to decide how credible you and your friend John are. When they check the information, they will go to Mr. Black anyway, so your source John is unimportant.

Most likely they will double-check the information. However, readers will not be pleased to have to track down your sources whether or not your information is correct. This is part of the writer's job. Outside of class work, if you presented unverified or unverifiable information (as the case with John) in this state, you will lose readers. People want to know they can trust the information provided by the writer to be the best authority possible for the situation.

Supporting Detail #2
Then provide a second specific, concrete example, using the model above but from a different source.

Supporting Detail #Whatever
You can have more than two supports, but not less. For instance, you might include a quote from a parent to show how broad the criticism of the bill has

reached, or politicians and teachers in other areas, or you might use two quotes from Senators and two from teachers to show criticism is not just from a rogue voice.

Concluding Statement for Paragraph #1
Why is this claim important to your thesis claim (reinforcing your claim to the thesis)?

Each paragraph should follow this pattern:

Your First Claim (that covers all the topics you will present in this paragraph):

Your Supporting Detail #1 (for one topic announced in your topic sentence):

Sandwich Quote #1:

Sandwich Quote #2:

Your Supporting Detail #2 (for the same topic for Detail #1):

Sandwich Quote #3:

Sandwich Quote #4:

_____

Your Concluding Statement (about why this
information is important to your
topic sentence):

*If you have included more than one topic in the paragraph
you will need two supporting detail for **each** topic. To re-
cap, for each sub-topic in your paper you must provide: 1-
topic sentence, 2-supporting details, 4-quotes to prove your
supporting details, and 1-concluding statement. The more
topics you want this paragraph to cover the more support
will be needed to be added to the paragraph. This is why
writing guides tell students to stick with only one topic per
body paragraph.*

Body Paragraph #2

A transition <u>and</u> Second claim that supports your
thesis: *Another reason that American schools are failing its
students is that teaching certification does not focus on the
administrative duties of a teacher or ensure more than five
college classes were passed by the person receiving the
license. Therefore, a person 'qualified' to teach English may
have a BA in math but earned Cs in five English classes.*

Transition: Before beginning your next point, you
will need to provide the reader with information
about how it fits into your grand scheme of things. In
the case above, I have connected this paragraph to a
preceding point with the words 'another reason'. This
phrase shows that it is not my first point, which could

either be my strongest or weakest point. However, the paragraph will provide added reasons why American schools are failing students. What is different here is the reason I am claim that the schools are failing.

Topic Sentence #2: In the topic sentence the next sub-topic needs to be presented.

Supporting Detail #1: Support the claim for this body paragraph.

Sandwich Quote: Provide evidence that scholars support this view. (The least amount of support you need here is one Sandwich Quote. Often it will not be enough unless you have found the leading expert on the topic.)

Transition Sentence: Connect your two supporting points together are the same (similarly, likewise, in comparison, indeed, moreover, in addition) or different (however, nevertheless, in contrast, conversely).

Supporting Detail #2: Support the claim for this body paragraph.

Sandwich Quote: Provide evidence that scholars support this view. (Again, one is the least, you can get away with but it must be an extremely authoritarian source. It is always better to put two quotes in.)

Concluding Statement: How does this information aid your cause?

Body Paragraph #3
___

A transition <u>and</u> Second claim that supports your thesis.

Transition:

Supporting Detail #1: Support the claim for this body paragraph.

    Sandwich Quote:

Transition:

Supporting Detail #2: Support the claim for this body paragraph.

    Sandwich Quote:

Concluding Statement:

Body Paragraph #4
___

A transition <u>and</u> Second claim that supports your thesis.

Transition:

Topic Sentence:

Supporting Detail #1: Support the claim for this body paragraph.

 Sandwich Quote:

Supporting Detail #2: Support the claim for this body paragraph.

 Sandwich Quote:

Concluding Statement:

Body Paragraphs ??

Continue on with **Transition and Statement that supports your thesis** until you have covered everything you need to cover. An essay has a minimum of three paragraphs, but there is no maximum. You must, however, continue until you have fully explained your claims by providing **examples and a concluding statement**.

There is no magic number to an essay, on number of **paragraphs or words. You must explain enough to show 1) that your claim is true and 2) you understand the material you are covering in your essay.**

Section 8: Wrapping It Up.

Conclusion

This part should 1) circle back to the introduction [I could mention the student again or the number of students' failed by the system] and 2) answer "So what?".

Ex. Due to "No Child Left Behind," inadequate teaching certification standards, and too much money diverted to pay school administrators instead of teachers, students, like B, are failed by the education system every year. [Restatement of my thesis and circle to opening to signal this work is coming to an end without saying "in conclusion."]

I might stress the need for a solution or what the audience could do to help stop the problem or the impact failed students have on the American economy as untrained workers who will be stuck in low-paying jobs, unable to pay the increasing tuition rates and unable to advance because they lack skills. This information must come from you. You cannot add sources here. However you sum it up, it must be part of what you know.

I could not propose a solution to this problem, in this paper. It is far too complex to be addressed in a conclusion—I would need an entire paper focused on possible solutions. As a student writer, it is unlikely you would have the authority to make a solution valid. You have no experience in administrating school policies, only experience with how they are implemented to affect you. Therefore, you are qualified to note there is a problem with a policy, but not likely to be believed if you say you have found the perfect solution for the problem. It is not that theoretically a student could not come up with a solution, but that they would not understand the rules and procedures for adopting new policies to make a solution workable, thus proving a solution is viable would need another paper with sources to verify the information.

First Name, Last Name of Writer

Name of Teacher

Name of Course

Date

Title

Hook.

XXXXXXXXXXXXXXXXXXXXXXXXXXXXXXXXXXXXXX

XXXXXXXXXXXXXXXXXXXXXXXXXXXXXXXXXXXXXX

XXXXXXXXXXXXXXXXXXXXXXXXXXXXXXXXXXXXXX

XXXXXXXXXXXXXXXXXXXXXXXXXXXXXXXXXXXXXX

XXXXXXXXXXBackground information about topic.

XXXXXXXXXXXXXXXXXXXXXXXXXXXXXXXXXXXX

XXXXXXXXXXXXXXXXXXXXXXXXXXXXXXXXXXXX

XXXXXXXXXXXXXXXXXXXXXXXXXXXXXXXXXXXX

Transition to thesis.

XXXXXXXXXXXXXXXXXXXXXXXXXXXXXXXX Thesis.

Briefly, More background, or First subtopic in topic sentence. XXXXXXXXXXXXX

XXXXXXXXXXXXXXXXXXXXXXXXXXXXXXXXXXXXXXXX

XXXXXXXXXXXXXXXXXXXXXXXXX

Supporting Detail explained.

XXXXXXXXXXXXXXXXXXXXXXXXXXXXXXXXX XXX

Sandwich Quote. According to Sam Smith, author of 26 novels, "XXXXXXXXXXXXXX

XXXXXXXXXXXXXXXXXXXXXXXXXXXXXX"

(citation). Summary of quote. XXXXXXX

XXXXXXXXX Transition. XXXXXXXXXXXXXXX.

Second Supporting Detail explained.

XXXXXXXXXXXXXXXXXXXXXXXXXXXXXXXXXXXXX

XXXXXXXXXXXXXXXXXXXXXXXXXXXXXXXX

Sandwich Quote. According to Raymond Chandler,

(citation). Summary of quote. XXXXXXXXXXXX

XXXXXXXXXXXXXXXXXXXXXXXXXXXXXXXXXXXXX

XXXXXXXXXXXXXXXXXXXXXXXXXConcluding

statement of why this point is important to major

claim.

Transition, Second subtopic in topic sentence.

XXXXXXXXXXXXXXXXXXXXXXXXXXXXXXXXXXXX

XXXXXXXXXX XXXXXXXXXXXXXXXXXXXXXXXX

Supporting Detail explained.

XXXXXXXXXXXXXXXXXXXXXXXXXXXXXXXXXX XXX

Sandwich Quote. According to Sam Smith, author of

26 novels, "XXXXXXXXXXXXXXX

XXXXXXXXXXXXXXXXXXXXXXXXXXXXXXXX"

(citation). Summary of quote. XXXXXXX

XXXXXXXXX Transition. XXXXXXXXXXXXXXXX.

Second Supporting Detail explained.

XXXXXXXXXXXXXXXXXXXXXXXXXXXXXXXXXXXXXX

XXXXXXXXXXXXXXXXXXXXXXXXXXXXXXXX

Sandwich Quote. According to Raymond Chandler,

famous mystery writer, "XXXXXXXXXXXXXXXXXX"

(citation). Summary of quote. XXXXXXXXXXXXX

XXXXXXXXXXXXXXXXXXXXXXXXXXXXXXXXXXXXXX

XXXXXXXXXXXXXXXXXXXXXXXXXConcluding

statement of why this point is important to major

claim.

Transition, third subtopic in topic sentence.

XXXXXXXXXXXXXXXXXXXXXXXXXXXXXXXXXXXXX

XXXXXXXXX XXXXXXXXXXXXXXXXXXXXXXXXX

Supporting Detail explained.

XXXXXXXXXXXXXXXXXXXXXXXXXXXXXXXXXXXXXXX

XXXXXXXXXXXXXXXXXXXXXXXXXXXXXX

Sandwich Quote. According to Sam Smith, author of

26 novels, "XXXXXXXXXXXXXXX

XXXXXXXXXXXXXXXXXXXXXXXXXXXXXX"

(citation). Summary of quote. XXXXXXX XXXXXXXXX

Transition. XXXXXXXXXXXXXXXX. Second

Supporting Detail explained.

XXXXXXXXXXXXXXXXXXXXXXXXXXXXXXXXXXXXXXXX

XXXXXXXXXXXXXXXXXXXXXXXXXXXXXXXX

Sandwich Quote. According to Raymond Chandler,

famous mystery writer, "XXXXXXXXXXXXXXXXX"

(citation). Summary of quote. XXXXXXXXXXXX

XXXXXXXXXXXXXXXXXXXXXXXXXXXXXXXXXXXXX

XXXXXXXXXXXXXXXXXXXXXXXConcluding

statement of why this point is important to major

claim.

Conclusion restatement of thesis in new words.

Reinforce why claim is important, explain So What?

Point to new research or possible solutions if

appropriate.

Have students fill out the template as a zero-draft project and assign points for its completion.

Encourage students to view writing as a process of change rather than a final product. The shift in point of view does not have to be labor intensive in grading. Students could be given a fixed number of points for just completing the tasks and the sections can be workshopped in peer review sessions for feedback.

Papers written in sections that have already been reviewed by the instructor are faster to grade than starting with new information for each essay.

As a teacher, you must decide whether the point of the class is to teach them to write or to punish them for not having mastered writing before they came to your class.

Chapter 3

Understanding Argument and the Standard Academic Essay

As discussed in the Overview in Chapter One, argument is often misunderstood by students. Students are told they should not argue, i.e. 'fight'. They carry this meaning over to their assignment. For these students being told to present an argument, means to take a belligerent stand on the topic, to be dogmatic, to crush the people who have different views and present them as stupid or ridiculous.

This interpretation of the word 'argument' is not the academic meaning of the term. In the academy the term argument is used to present a point of view with reasoned examples. The argument paper is considered part of an on-going conversation among scholars about a particular topic. It is part of an intellectual discussion in which all points of view are considered and discussed until a best solution is found. (At least theoretically or ideally. Some scholars and teachers bash those with different viewpoints, regardless of the common endorsement that academia encourages and supports differences. Just try bringing up support for the right to carry concealed weapons on a university or college campus and see how much diversity is valued.)

This chapter will cover the meaning of argument in detail.

A claim is not a thesis, but thesis can be a claim.

All good arguments begin with claims; therefore, it is necessary to understand what a claim is, what it is not, and how to make one.

To begin with a claim is different from a thesis. A thesis does not have to focus on persuading someone to do something or believe something. Moreover, the thesis is often broader in scope than a claim, as a thesis must only focus the reader on the topic and identify the main idea. A claim, however, must take a position.

A Thesis	A Claim
• Focuses audience on topic and main idea	• Persuades audience
• Does not have to offer point of view or position	• Is a position
• Conveys an idea,	• Based on a belief

impression, or opinion	about an issue
• Not necessary to have only credible sources	• Only credible sources can be used

The differences can be seen in this example:

> **Thesis:** Economic policies continue to be a hotly debated issue in American political circles.
>
> **Claim:** Because economic policies are being debated rather than acted on, America will continue to experience rising unemployment rates.

The difference between a claim and a thesis is a central one to all students. A thesis can be used for any level work, but generally only a claim can be produced for top quality work. A claim must govern all journal publication, honors, thesis, and dissertation work.

Types of Claims.

There are several types of statements that can be made into arguments:

> ➢ Statements of fact- a debatable claim that something is or is not true.
> ➢ Statements of policy- a claim that something should or should not be true.

This is a claim that a solution will or will not work in a given context.

➢ Statements of value-a claim that something does or does not have value or worth. This is a claim centered on evaluations of a situation.

➢ Statement of definition- a claim that offers a definition different from popular understanding or current meanings associated with it.

➢ Statement of cause- a claim that argues an event or a series of events created a situation.

Arguments Involve Uncertainty.

Students new to argument can find it difficult to understand why they are being asked to write about things that are not certain. How can people show they are learned if the information they write about may not be true? This, however, is the heart of the academy.

A brief history here might help explain some things. Plato and Aristotle were walking around the Forum in Athens. Plato began the walks. He would stop there among the crowds and discuss things with passersby. Mostly he talked about the meaning of life, what it means to have moral values, who should be allowed to be officials, why we are on earth, and things of this type. One of his students, of the many who followed Plato around in case he said something rummy or juicy, was Aristotle. Aristotle wrote down the brilliant things his teacher said, and his own brilliant ideas. Aristotle went one step further. Instead of walking around hoping to attract brilliant students, Aristotle started a school. It was known as the Academy, which is why ever since all schools are referred to generally as academies.

Among the many topics that interested these two men were rhetoric and oratory. Public speech making was an essential skill at the time since most people were not literate, meaning they could not read or write. Rhetoric took in many topics. It was a sort of umbrella term for many critical thinking skills, including math and science.

During the Middle Ages, long, long after Plato and Aristotle had killed over, rhetoric became more associated with public speech making (still a key player in a world that had few people who could read and write) and the structure of written works. During this time the patterns determined by Plato and Aristotle for spectacular public speeches became the norm for written works.

So, to make a long story short, argument began on the streets of Athens. It was not a form to discuss what everyone knew, but what they did not know, things like our purpose in life. It was focused on how best to present uncertainties. It was also used to show how assumptions and beliefs can be made to motivate people to help us and believe the same things we do. However, manipulating people was a side-product, often frowned up. The really, core goal was to talk about what we do not know in order to find out if we do know something after all, if that makes sense.

An argument must contain uncertainty; therefore, you must be care in choosing a statement of fact.

Not an argument-

James O. Born wrote *Field of Fire*.

The Spanish Flu claimed many lives throughout the decade from 1910 to 1920.

Shakespeare died in 1616.

Van Gogh painted *Starry Night*.

Stem cell research receives government and private funding.

Pit bulls are considered a safety concern by many people.

Universities and colleges make money on banks market credit cards towards college students.

There is no uncertainty in these statements; they are facts.

Students seem to have the most difficulty crafting a statement of fact. All statements of fact cannot be used as an argument (see the box above). Any fact will not do. The reason for this difficulty is that all statements of fact used in an argument must be things that other people may disagree with to varying degrees. The statements of fact in the box above, however, are statements that no one can dispute: Born did write and publish the book *Field of Fire*, the Spanish Flu was the worst epidemic during the turn of the century and did kill many people during the second decade of the 20th century, Shakespeare did die in 1616, Van Gogh did paint the well-known picture *Starry Night*, stem cell research does receive funding, many people are concerned about the in-bred traits of pit bulls, and higher education does receive a cut of the debit you incur in pursuing degrees. All of these issues end immediately upon someone providing the research to document these events.

That does not mean statements of fact can never be questioned. For instance, if we were to state 'Shakespeare wrote 19 plays.' This seems like a simple statement of fact; however, many scholars dispute whether or not Shakespeare actually wrote the plays that bear his name. Some believe that Francis Bacon wrote the plays and had Shakespeare, a theater owner produce the plays. These scholars believe that the sensitive political nature of the plays would justify someone else, better known as a scholar in his own day, to have hidden his identity to avoid ending up as a political prisoner in the Tower of London. Others believe that Christopher Marlow, another playwright, actually wrote the plays while he was in hiding in Italy and sent them back to Shakespeare to produce because Marlow is widely reputed to have been a spy and they believe spies fake their own deaths. Still others believe that a member of the aristocracy wrote the plays and allowed Shakespeare to publish them because public censure forbad people from seeking praise, although this type of censure only remained in effect for women during this time period.

Because of these scholarly debates over who Shakespeare was and why he wrote and produced his plays, the statement of fact that 'Shakespeare wrote 19 plays' involves uncertainty.

For some of the statements above I can create uncertainty. For example, instead of saying 'Pit bulls are considered a safety concern by some people,' I could rephrase my statement to say, 'Despite recent concerns, pit bulls are not dangerous pets,' or conversely, 'Despite the assurances of breeders and enthusiasts, pit bulls are dangerous pets to own.'

First, to make this statement arguable I have placed the danger in more context. I have suggested the pit bull is a dangerous pet, not that the dog is inherently more vicious than other type dog. Indeed, most of the concern has been over the debate whether people should be allowed to purchase the dogs as household pets as several children have been attacked by them. There is no question over whether or not they make more dangerous guard dogs than say a German shepherd.

Second, I have taken a side in the issue. In on claim I have registered my support for those who think pit bulls make fine pets; in the other claim I have registered my disapproval for the selling of the dog as a pet.

The variables 'pet', 'are not dangerous', and 'are dangerous' provide enough controversy for a paper.

In this case, the statement is not so much a statement of fact but a statement of opinion. The fact that the statement is based upon an opinion does not justify the use of statements 'I think' or 'I feel' or 'I believe.' As stated in an earlier chapter, the 'I' is reserved for those with years of work studying a particular thing or field. Students do not have the experience necessary to claim this 'I' voice since they have not worked in the field; therefore, a student should not base their entire argument on their personal beliefs, values, or concerns.

tudents need to learn how to phrase opinions into acceptable academic arguments.

ps:

- Never phrase an opinion in a personal way ('I think', 'I believe', 'I feel.') It is considered disrespectful to scholars.
- Use qualifiers to strengthen the controversy.
  - Use words like *may, necessarily, frequently, in most cases, probably, if/then, often, almost, some, usually, likely, many, most, maybe.*
  - *Example*: Marijuana may not be as addictive as other drugs, but legalizing it does not make it a safe drug.
- Avoid bi-polar debates.
  - Avoid words like *all, best, every, never*, none, *worst*.
  - *Example:* All student athletes believe steroids can be used safely. This is an exaggerated opinion and impossible to support.
- Concede alternative points of view.
  - Use words like *even though, while it is true, some believe, admittedly, granted.*

Most importantly, argument is a decision-making tool. Although it is often misperceived to be quarrelsome and unpleasant, argument is about giving reasons. These reasons justify and support the claim being made, which, in turn, show how the writer thinks and what the writer bases assumptions on.

Without learning the ability to support or claims with reasons, people would have make decisions based on whims and fancies, or commands and dictates. Either people would agree because they like us or because they are afraid of us or what we could do to them.

However with an understanding of argument, we can appeal to an audiences' reason. This implies concern for the audience. We do not want to rely on their blind trust in us or bully them into a position. By providing arguments, we allow them to arrive at their own informed decisions because we have informed them of what sources we consider credible and valid.

To have an effective argument, does rely on the assent of the audience it is true. After all, we want people to join our causes and be part of what we believe in, but we also want them to understand our behavior. Still, the audience can simply be made aware of how and why others think differently than themselves for an argument to be successful at another level. Providing reasons, can be the basis of understanding different ideas and cultures.

Thus, argument becomes a basis for decision-making. As an audience, we determine who we will align with based upon how people present their arguments and the reasons they provide for their position.

We use arguments every day of our lives. You will need to take this skill with you everywhere you go. Whether you are responding to an article for class, becoming part of a team at work, blogging, tweeting, or managing others in the workplace, you will need this skill to be taken seriously by providing credible information through a variety of emotional, logical, and ethical appeals. You want to present yourself as both well informed on the subject and sensitive to the beliefs of the other side.

Argument Can Be Either Inductive or Deductive.

There are two ways to form an argument using different types of reasoning: inductive and deductive.

Inductive.

This is the model of most everyday thinking. The conclusion relies on probability to prove that it is possible, not that it is the only conclusion. In this method, you will make generalizations based on a specific number of examples. That is, you will provide examples and then draw conclusions from these examples.

For instance, if you were late to work on different occasions and eight were due to problems with your vehicle, you could conclude that the probability is you will need to find more reliable transportation before you are fired. The examples come first and are analyzed to reach a common consensus among the information. Here, the reason you were late varied, but most of the incidents involved car maintenance problems. You can exclude over-sleeping and traffic the most serious reform in getting to work on time. Buying an alarm clock and leaving early may be simpler solutions, but they will not substantially alter the fact that you are arriving to work late, as they only improve your circumstances 20% of the time, whereas finding more reliable transportation will improve the problem 80% of the time.

Deductive.

In deductive reasoning our conclusions follow from our premise. Indeed, the conclusion contains nothing not discussed in the premises that supported our claim. Deductive reasoning assumes a general principle or claim and then applies it to a particular case. Typically this general principle is arrived at by induction, and the knowledge of how the world generally behaves.

Behavior analysts use deductive methods to determine who is more likely to have committed a behavior. Take serial killers. Most identified, tried, and convicted serial killers are white men, between the ages of 20-40, most had issues dealing with women due to having a controlling mother. When a behavior analyst is told there have been three victims (three being the least number of people killed by one person to be classified as a serial killer) with similar MOs (motive of operations), that analyst will know that most people captured who committed this particular type of crime are white men between the ages 20-40. Hence, they will advise local police to check white men between the ages of 20-40. That does not mean the actual killer is not Hispanic or Black. Only that the probability based upon known cases would suggest a white man. This profile created by the analyst would then have to be applied to each suspect to see if it remains accurate — that is the police will use deductive reasoning by examining each suspect based on the profile provided.

Each of these methods is based on three types of appeals: emotional, logical, and ethical. Traditionally, these methods do not act independently, but as a collection of resources to influence an audience.

Emotional Appeals.

The emotional appeal relies on stirring passions, making people care about something. Many students view this as negative; however, it is not. It is like the hook a student needs to provide in order to get a reader to continue reading. The hook provides an emotional response to make the reader concerned or interested in finding out about a topic. For instance, most people do not care about bees. They exist as part of a world we no longer take an active interest in—the natural world, yet there are other people passionately interested in bees. If one of those passionate people writes about bees in a way that invites us to enter their world, the reader will join that writer's passion and learn about bees. It is not the subject, it is the emotion we bring to our writing that matters.

Any writing entirely devoid of passion and emotion is not worth the effort of producing. No one will want to read it. However, emotion cannot be the only foundation for our writing.

Logical Appeals.

Logical appeals have the most trust because we believe they are impartial, almost scientific in application. We believe that they are bias free and objectively presented. The highest order of logical appeals is facts. We believe that facts will always be facts and that by examining them we can check others evaluations of them.

Facts are not, however, the only type of logical appeal. We can learn first-hand evidence from observations and interviews. That is from seeing the world and by talking to people.

Similarly, we can learn from surveys and questionnaires. This is collecting large quantities of data to test our observations and check information in interviews. This type of logical appeal has a broader base and allows us to check our information in different settings.

There is also experiments and personal experience. This group is broader still. For a survey, you would draw up a list of questions and hand them out, collect the data, compile charts and graphs, and reach conclusions. With an experiment, you would research the question, conduct a formal study with a blind group of participants, and discuss the variables that affected your study. With a survey, you do not have a blind group that is observed.

For instance, if you are testing a new drug, you would have one group that received a fake pill (the blind group), one that received the drug, and one group that did not take a pill. Some people in the blind group may believe they have improved because they took a pill. The test results of the actual pill would have to be weight among the results of those who improved taking the medicine, those who believed they improved or showed signs of improving by taking the fake medication, and those who improved without any pill.

Finally, there is second-hand knowledge. Experience gained by other people that we can count on to help support our own beliefs and claims based on the experiences of others that has been validated, statistics, and evidence drawn by authorities.

Ethical Appeals.

There is always an ethical element to writing, and most particularly to writing arguments. The core goals are not only to provide information but to have people act on the information we provide. If for instance we put up a blog and write an article for it on how to take a picture, we expect those who search out our blog to follow the advice we have provided. That is, we have asked them to set aside their own ideas and beliefs to follow ours. Although having set aside their beliefs to follow our directs on taking a picture is not monumental in and of itself, it is still putting a limit on someone else's choices by suggesting the blogger is a superior force that should out-weigh the audience's own beliefs and ideas.

No matter the issue, argument and writing itself attempts to influence people. Even this book attempts to influence, I want to influence the way you compose essays. Influencing people is not evil or bad. If you want an allowance or a raise, you will have to influence someone to get it. If you want a car, you will have to influence someone for this too. If you want dinner, you will have to influence someone. Influencing others does not, nor should it be, a form of brainwashing. It is simply explaining why you need a raise, a car, or your dinner.

Argument should not influence people against their will, but seek a freewill choice of agreement from which to work. This is the heart of a democracy. We set aside some differences in order to achieve things for the greater good of all. Unlike living under an autocratic tyrant, we choose what to set aside by votes and consensus; someone else's rules are not imposed on us without our collective voice being heard. Thus, argument respects different ways of thinking and reasoning.

Individual Arguments Include a Claim, Evidence, and Inference Linking the Evidence to the Claim, and a Warrant Justifying the Inference.

As shown below in the table, the credibility of sources is important as this information supports the evidence. By building up the evidence, you prove that something is likely or possible. Once that information has been established, you can provide the inference, or your analysis of why the information is important. These are the grounds upon which your claim is based.

However, the evidence must be balanced by warrants. While your inference is the main line leading to between the evidence and the claim, the warrant is the license to make the inference, or assumption. If the connection between the evidence and the inference is not clear or may have more than one possibility than each warrant, or assumption, must be supported and established with more information for the audience.

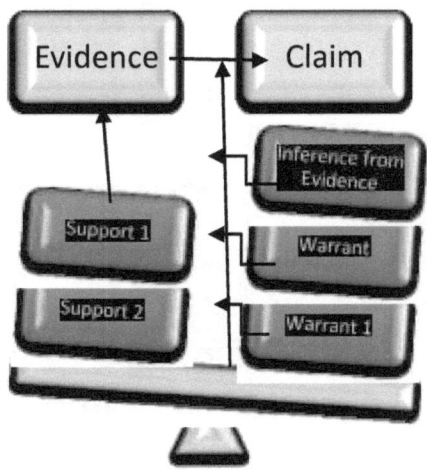

In this manner, each item you introduce into your paper is placed on a balance. If you do not provide adequate supports to prove it is true than your balance tilts to one side and your paper is harmed by the deficit.

In a well presented argument, the claim would out-weigh the evidence.

Patterns and the Order of Things.

Arguments can be arranged in many forms, focusing on the part to the whole. Indeed, most of the writing genres can be incorporated to inform an argument. Support can be accomplished with extended examples or illustrations from which we can learn about others by applying the individual case as a selection of how typical people or events mirror the same issues.

This is true of classification as well. By understanding a group we can make assumptions about how people or things in the group will behave.

Far more likely is the use of comparison, in which we explain why things should be treated alike. We can use analogies that are either figurative, a comparison or relationships, or literal, a direct comparison.

Direct comparisons are easy to understand. For instance, we can compare our attempts to obtain a national healthcare plan with that of England.

There is, however, a judicial analogy that falls under a direct comparison that may not be as easy to understand. The judicial analogy is a special case; it sets a precedent for the matter at hand. It is sometimes used as a rule of conduct. Because someone has begun this pattern, all similar cases should be understood in the same way.

Figurative analogies are less easily understood. For example, if someone compares a government to a house. The two items do not have the same sphere of reality. However, we can make the comparison once we have established that a house had someone who is the head (President), there are other people in the house who have to be considered (Senate, House of Representatives, Supreme Court). In order for the household to function, some compromise is necessary (balance of power).

Arguments can also be made in the form of causes and effects. Causal factors assert that one factor has influence over another.

Lastly, arguments can be made with commonplaces, that is, things that are based on social knowledge. Commonplaces are beliefs and judgments audiences will generally accept because they are part of the same culture. For example, the question 'are you better off today than you were four years ago?' In an on-going recession most people will answer 'no.'

Each person may not have tallied up how much they make, how the money has been off-set by inflation, or how much time they spend on the job. Due to a general sense of hard times appearing in the news and stories by other people, they will state no, they are not better off now than they were four years before.

Maintaining Status Quo and Attacking and Defending.

Arguments can take many forms: personal, technical, or social.

Unfortunately, for those who insist on using 'I', the attack may become personal. The writer who uses 'I' invites others to question and destroy the beliefs that person holds dear. In this instance, the argument becomes of importance to the person who wrote it because the evaluations directly reflect that person, not generally held assumptions.

Typically, the well-crafted academic argument will be of concern for the technical field. Attacks will remain on general theories, not on particular people who may or may not believe them. This argument is conditioned by background and expertise in the field. The ideas are accessible to all who have access to the field, and, therefore, all members of the field will be able to advance a theory for the benefit of the field.

Within the technical field will be a group of experts who may be subdivided into their own group due to their special knowledge of the problems facing that field.

Increasingly school taut social action when learning to write arguments. Social action means that the writer wants someone to do something with the information they have written. Teachers will assign papers on a subject like immigration and expect students to participate in movements for this cause, as was seen in recent cases in Texas and California in which students left school and marched in the streets in protest of possible government actions to remove illegal and undocumented workers from business and deport them back to their country of origin.

Arguments in the public sphere are concerned with matters that affect society in their role as citizens. In general, the argument is open to all, whether the writer is a member of that society or not.

There is generally no clear divide between these areas. Abortion may be seen as a public sphere issue, but it may also be seen as personal.

Credible Evidence.

Credible evidence falls into several categories:

Testimony-this can be personal experience, recorded information provided by an expert in the field, or documented statements collected by experts.

Examples-consists of specific instances of a general claim.

Statistics-numerical data, usually taken from studies, that prove tendency for something to occur.

Tangible objects-ancient manuscripts, photographs, old census records, foundations of buildings can all be placed in this category. We can prove things to be true by physical remains. For example, many claimed that the ancient city of Babylon did not really exist; however, the city was unearthed and Biblical archeologists could point to the writings and say it did exist.

Social consensus-this is where beliefs function as facts. Shared values, believed history, previously established conclusions and core values promoted by a society are all types of social consensus. In the Middle Ages it was a social consensus that it was acceptable for girls as young as thirteen to marry. Today's social consensus believes girls should be at least eighteen unless there are unusual circumstances surrounding the event, even then the youngest age acceptable is fifteen.

Bibliography Kamhi-Stein, L.D. "Redesigning the Writing Assignment in General Education Courses." <u>College</u> <u>ESL</u> 7.1 (1997): 49-61.

Have students collect advertisements, either print copies or those on the web, and have them try to find as many types of appeals in the ads they can. Teams can be formed with scores kept on each team.

Have students bring in five newspaper stories they think can be used to create an argument. Select articles to discuss as a class. Have students meet in groups to discuss how they would develop an argument from their stories.

Give students a set of facts and have them write a brief paper using the inductive method, then the deductive method to organize the data.

Have students 'treasure hunt' credible sources using internet web

www.ingramcontent.com/pod-product-compliance
Lightning Source LLC
Chambersburg PA
CBHW020247290526
45784CB00003B/1139